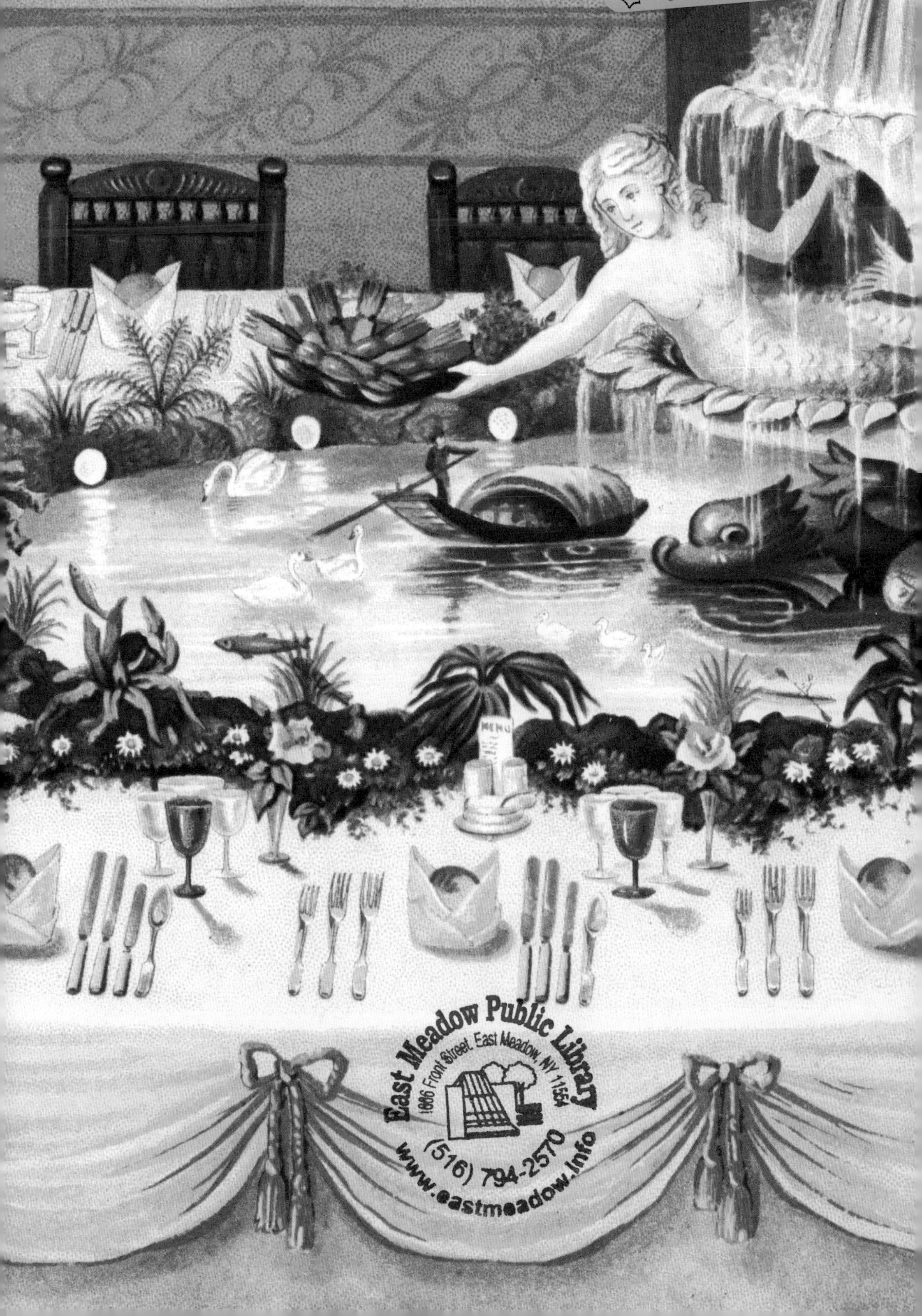

FOOD FIGHTS & CULTURE WARS

# TOM NEALON

# FOOD

# FIGHTS

# CULTURE

# & WARS

## A SECRET HISTORY OF TASTE

THE OVERLOOK PRESS

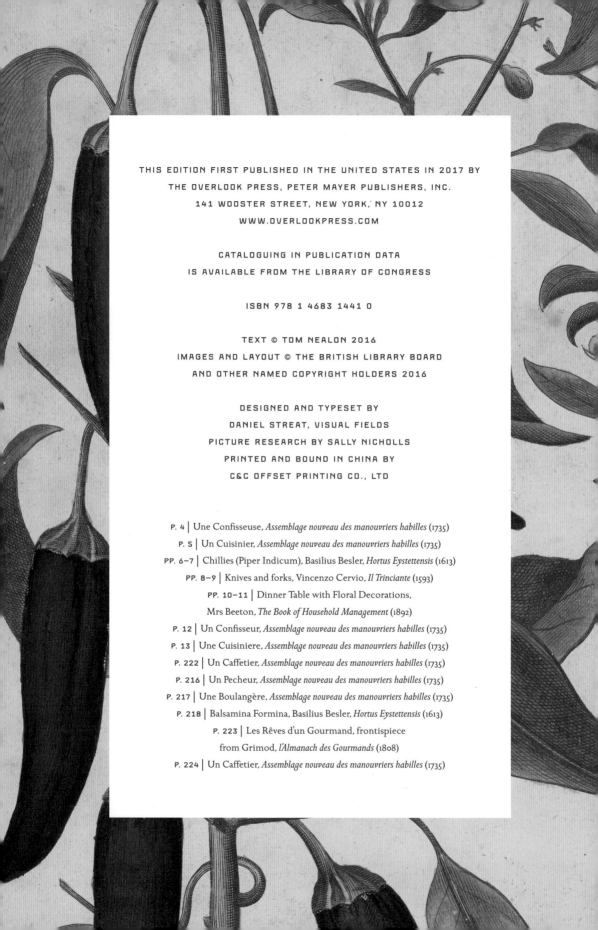

THIS EDITION FIRST PUBLISHED IN THE UNITED STATES IN 2017 BY
THE OVERLOOK PRESS, PETER MAYER PUBLISHERS, INC.
141 WOOSTER STREET, NEW YORK, NY 10012
WWW.OVERLOOKPRESS.COM

CATALOGUING IN PUBLICATION DATA
IS AVAILABLE FROM THE LIBRARY OF CONGRESS

ISBN 978 1 4683 1441 0

TEXT © TOM NEALON 2016
IMAGES AND LAYOUT © THE BRITISH LIBRARY BOARD
AND OTHER NAMED COPYRIGHT HOLDERS 2016

DESIGNED AND TYPESET BY
DANIEL STREAT, VISUAL FIELDS
PICTURE RESEARCH BY SALLY NICHOLLS
PRINTED AND BOUND IN CHINA BY
C&C OFFSET PRINTING CO., LTD

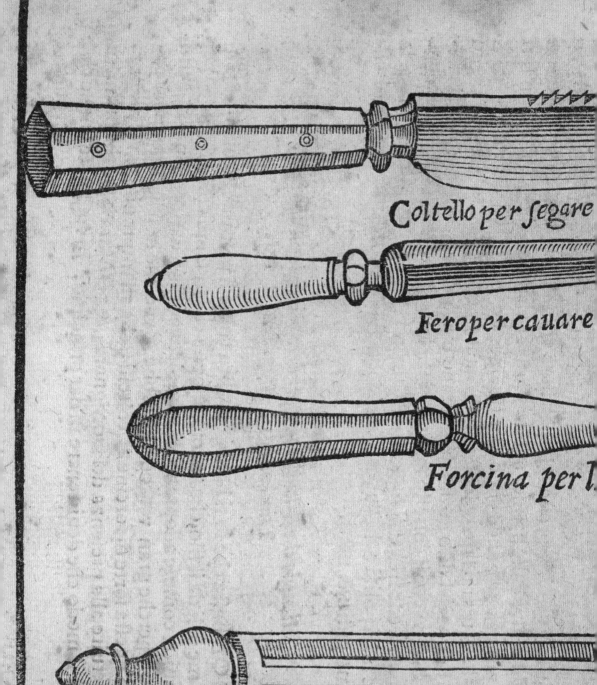

Coltello per fegare

Fero per cauare

Forcina per l.

Fero per tr

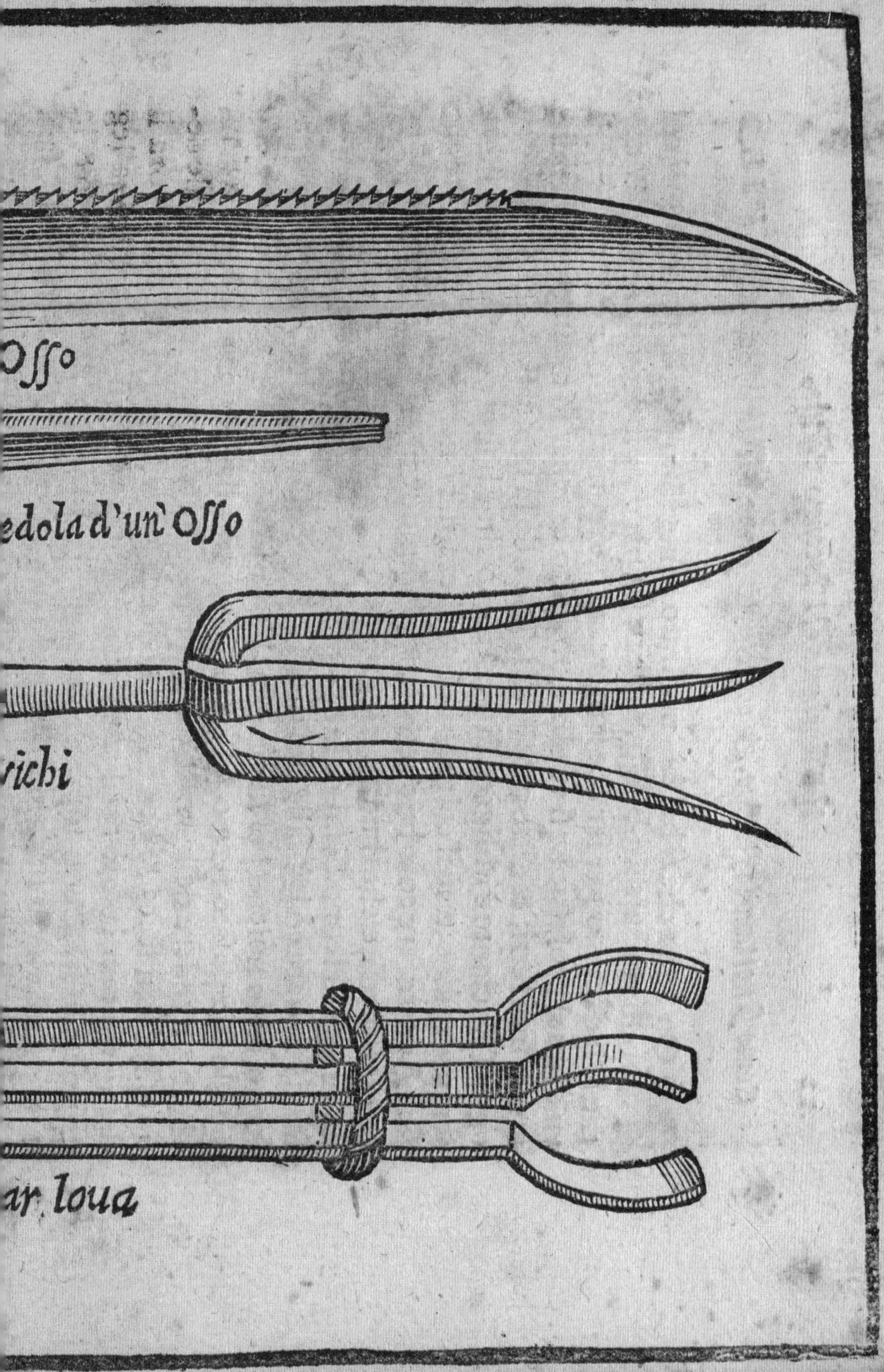

Osso

edola d'un' Osso

richi

ar loua

# CONTENTS

**CHAPTER SEVEN**

**CHAPTER THREE**

**CHAPTER TEN**

**CHAPTER ONE**

**CHAPTER FOUR**

**CHAPTER NINE**

**CHAPTER TWO**

**CHAPTER FIVE**

**CHAPTER SIX**

**CHAPTER EIGHT**

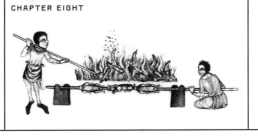

# INTRODUCTION

As fond as I am of eating, from the beginning it was the lies and artifice of food that grabbed me. About ten years ago, I had the idea to try to cook every food mentioned in Geoffrey Chaucer's *The Canterbury Tales* (c. 1390). I think it arose from my interest in the scurrilous cook Roger, who would drain gravy out of pies to sell in the lucrative second-hand gravy market, but also that I had ended a run of bad restaurant jobs to open my used bookshop in Boston, Massachusetts, and I wanted to splice these two lives together. One of the first dishes that I cooked in preparation for my project was a thirteenth-century recipe for chicken, that was first taken off the bone, the bone cleaned and boiled, and, finally, the chicken rewrapped around the bone and fried in place to achieve chicken disguised to look like chicken.

I've long had a dilettante's interest in the food of the Late Middle Ages – that is, from around 1300 to 1500. The food of these times is so foreign to our own: turtledoves, mutton, flagons of mead, and pork fat, which seems to appear in every dish. The cuisine was loaded with experimental oddities from the spice trade, and in a constant state of flux. I cooked a weird proto-blancmange held together with rice starch and almond milk, and a mashed-up pork dish called *mortorio*, a recipe from a fourteenth-century manuscript. However, my attempts to find a peacock to skin, roast, and then present with the skin replaced so that it appeared as though I was serving a live, if motionless, peacock on a platter, were stymied by the fact that it is apparently illegal to kill peacocks. I tried Miami, where peacocks run free through residential neighbourhoods, but was unable to bring myself to choke one to death. After cooking and writing about dozens of dishes from early cookbooks, and holding a few memorably strange dinner parties, I began to nurse a more general interest in the history of food. As my business succumbed to the pressure of the Internet and became less about selling used paperbacks than finding old and rare books, I began to buy the best examples I could find, with the (vague) intention of issuing a catalogue of rare early cookbooks.

Despite its central importance in our lives, the historical record of food is very patchy. In the ancient world there is just one cookbook that survived, from around the fourth century, and some rather random texts that describe banquets (the Ancient Greek Athenaeus' *The Learned Banqueters* from the late-second century

C.E., and a few other minor examples). During the Renaissance, between the fourteenth to seventeenth centuries, meals eaten by the European elite began to be recorded in cookbooks, but there are huge gaps in the accounts, even regarding what royalty was eating at the time. In the rise and fall of empires, the daily story of eating was very often neglected, even though discovery, exploitation, and speculation were so often food-related; as in colonial enterprises such as the spice trade, sugar plantations, and turkey-relocation programmes. A (very small) war was fought over the clove supply on Ambon Island in 1623, and while history records the war, there is no mention of why cloves, beyond their monetary value, were so beloved as to justify killing people. Diarists and historians such as Samuel Pepys (1633–1703) or John Evelyn (1620–1706) occasionally made valuable observations about what they and their contemporaries were eating, or about the opening of new restaurants, but even they give a very incomplete picture of what food was being eaten and what it meant to people. Food was everywhere and nowhere, lost in its own ubiquitous utility.

As a result, fanciful stories sprang up to explain from where these new foods

had come. The cooks usually had no idea of the truth and were fabricating origins long after the fact, and often with a surfeit of whimsy, so that these inventions are frequently described as delightful accidents: mayonnaise was invented to mimic thickened cream at a banquet; chocolate blew into a meat stew and created the Mexican dish *mole*; fresh cheese was abandoned in a cave and became Roquefort; coffee beans were discovered after herders observed their goats eating some and becoming frisky; and the Napoleon pastry was invented to outdo Beef Wellington (actually, that last one might be from Woody Allen's film *Love and Death*, 1975). Because food, especially prepared food, had never been consistently recorded, it had been relegated to a fictional universe outside history.

I figured that the most sensible plan was to go back to the source. Yet what I

OPPOSITE | *A Boke of Kokery* (c. 1440). Held at the British Library, this is one of about fifty medieval recipe manuscripts still in existence. The first recipe, shown here, is for 'Hare in Wortes [Herbs]'. | ABOVE | Preparing a banquet, from The Luttrell Psalter (1325–40).

found in the cookbooks was even weirder and less structured than I had anticipated. Since the twentieth century, we have come to expect that recipes will provide precise measurements and timings, and that the dishes have not only been attempted, but refined and perfected, by the writer. Such expectations are unhelpful when dealing with the first four centuries or so of the printed cookbook.

The very first printed cookbook – published in 1475, not long after the Gutenberg Bible, *c.* 1454 – announces what we should expect. Bartolomeo Sacchi's (1421–81) *De honesta voluptate et valetudine* ('On right pleasure and good health') is composed almost entirely of untested recipes cribbed from Maestro Martino da Como's (born *c.* 1430) *Liber de arte coquinaria* ('Book of the art of cooking'). Martino da Como was the most famous chef of the Western world in the fifteenth century, whereas Sacchi, known as Il Platina,

was, in fact, not even a cook: just an itinerant humanist with some publishing connections at the Vatican (he also wrote a papal history). Il Platina added to Martino's recipes advice on diet and medicine from classical sources to create a comprehensive book about food. The fifteenth century only saw this published and, in 1498, a printing of the fourth-century Roman manuscript cookery written by Apicius, *De re coquinaria* ('On the subject of cooking'), but the sixteenth century ushered in a strange melange of books on diet, medicinal food, and books of secrets.

The book of secrets had a long history in manuscript form, as people from the dawn of writing tried to keep record

LEFT | Clove Tree, 'Zacharias Wagener, A short account of the Voyages of Z.W. perform'd in thirty-five years', collected in Churchill, *A Collection of Voyages and Travels, Vol.2,* (1732). | ABOVE | Chillies, from Basilius Besler, *Hortus Eystettensis* (1613), the most magnificent botanical book ever made. | OPPOSITE Marx Rumpolt, *Ein new Kochbuch* (1604).

of tricks and recipes for such everyday tasks as making paint pigment, cleaning textiles, or mixing perfume, but also for creating aphrodisiacs, plague cures, and making sausages. The notion behind these books that the world could be better understood by travelling around and observing and cataloguing its phenomena, had a huge impact on the science of the Enlightenment in eighteenth-century Europe. Two of the most popular secret books were *The Secrets of the Reverend Maister Alexis of Piemont* by Girolamo Ruscelli, first published in Italian in 1555 and reprinted in profusion (in French in 1557, and in English in 1558) for over two hundred years, and a book of secrets by the French apothecary and prophet Michel de Nostredame (1503–66), or Nostradamus, also published in 1555, in Lyon. Before becoming famous for his prophecies, Nostradamus collected recipes for his book of secrets, which featured an entire section on jams and jellies, including a ridiculously complicated and exotic jam devised to be so delicious that it would make a woman fall in love with you. The popularity of secret books was such that it took some time before cookery and secrets became disentangled, making it difficult to discern whether food or medicine was the more pressing concern in sixteenth-century Europe.

One would have expected the sixteenth century to have produced a proliferation of written recipes featuring the new ingredients flowing into Europe from the Americas. The potato, tomato, chilli pepper, pumpkin, turkey, corn, and all those New World beans (that is, almost all beans, except soy, fava, and chickpea, or garbanzo) made their way to Europe during the 1500s, but had remarkably little impact on the recipes in printed cookbooks. What happened? Some of the new bounty just didn't find immediate

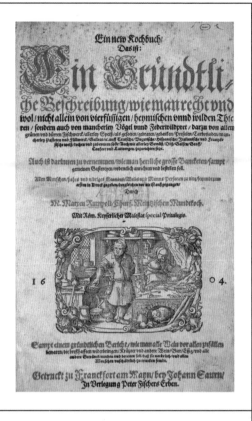

popularity: beans seemed mysterious, tomato and potato plants were refused because they are nightshades and were suspected of being as poisonous as the well-known European nightshades such as mandrake and belladonna were. European farmers were not completely mistaken on this point: all nightshades do have high (though not dangerously high, with respect to the edible plants) alkaloid content. The most famous of these alkaloids is nicotine, present in high quantities in tobacco, and in lower quantities in some nightshade foods such as tomato, potato, and aubergine, or eggplant (which is from Asia, but was adopted late in northern Europe). Corn, so popular in the Americas, was slow to catch on across the Atlantic, as Europeans already ate wheat, oats, rice, and barley. Chilli peppers, also from the nightshade family, were a little too powerful for

ABOVE & OPPOSITE | Plates from Bartolomeo Scappi's *Opera di M. Bartolomeo Scappi* (1570), depicting the medieval kitchen at work.

European palates (though adopted with alacrity in Asia when introduced there by Portuguese explorers). The turkey alone was a big hit, but even that had to compete with a wide range of domestic fowl. However, one of the first great modern cookbooks, *Opera* (1570), by famous Italian Renaissance chef Bartolomeo Scappi (*c.* 1500–1577), does contain a delightful recipe for pumpkin and cheese pie.

We forget, accustomed as we are to a wide variety of foods, that eating was a very serious matter of trial and error in the past. The crops that were planted in Europe were the end result of thousands of years of domestication, and the penalty for eating the wrong thing was very often sickness or death. However, beyond Scappi and the great German cookery *Ein new Kochbuch* ('A new cookbook'), written by Marx Rumpolt in 1581, most of the other cookbooks published in the sixteenth century were the same weird mixture of plagiarized recipes and diet books from ancient sources, with no mention of new ingredients. Which is not to say that they weren't influential – *Epulario*, a retread of Martino's recipes published in Venice in 1516 (and reprinted well into the seventeenth century) was, unlike Il Platina's earlier work, translated into English as *The Italian Banquet* in 1598, and included a recipe for baking a reinforced pie crust into which you could insert, through a hole in the bottom, two dozen live blackbirds (there was no disclaimer for any nose-biting that might ensue). Over the centuries, cookbooks were translated, and their influence crossed and re-crossed borders, but they didn't necessarily carry the same meaning from place to place. What did French food mean in Italy, where it held sway from the mid-seventeenth to the early-nineteenth century? French chef and patissier Jules Gouffé's enormously popular *Le Livre de*

*Cuisine* ('The book of cuisine', 1868) was translated into every European language, but it meant something different everywhere. It was a foreign cookbook in the Netherlands; an elucidation for Marie-Antoine Carême (1784–1833), a celebrity chef of the new French *grande cuisine* in Italy; and in Mexico it gained a section on Mexican cuisine and became the cookery bible for the upper-middle classes. Western cookbooks vaguely followed new ingredients, reflecting their speed and popularity, but how were the ingredients themselves faring?

As I waded through these books, tracing the history of various ingredients from inception to popularity to neglect to complete disappearance, I saw how strange and complex these old books seemed under scrutiny, how shifting and sybaritic was the detail that emerged. Some ingredients spread like wildfire: during the Middle Ages, almonds and sugar were imported from the Middle East

and suddenly appeared in every (upper-class) recipe, while saffron proliferated so rapidly that it was as though there were a royal decree that food be yellow. Some struggled to appear at all – the beloved tomato didn't appear until the 1680s, and it was well into the eighteenth century before it was used with regularity. So much of what happens with food is never written down, never immortalized: all the evidence eaten, forgotten.

Though most cookbooks were written by men, the great majority of cooking was done by women. Centuries of cookery were shrouded in dumb ignorance and misogyny: how many great cooks and great dishes have been rendered invisible to history, how many brilliant advances,

OPPOSITE | A kitchen illustrated in Christoforo di Messisbugo, *Banchetti compositioni di vivande, et apparecchio generale* (1549). | ABOVE | The resulting banquet, from the same volume.

cookeries (often by women), and the first American cookbook. In England, Hannah Glasse's (1708–70) *The Art of Cookery Made Plain and Easy* (1747) and Elizabeth Raffald's (1733–81) *The Experienced English Housekeeper* (1769) were especially important, carving out a place for British food and setting the stage for Mrs Isabella Beeton's (1836–65) bestselling *Book of Household Management* (1861), which compiled existing recipes with instructions for running an orderly Victorian bourgeois household.

All of these cookbooks tell a story, but it is so varied by class, gender, race, and geography that there are more holes than substance. There is most often no mention at all of the origins of the dishes or ingredients, and when there is, it is just as likely to be an invention. The famous French author Alexandre Dumas (1802–70) must have felt this was so, as his *Grand Dictionnaire de Cuisine* ('Grand kitchen dictionary', 1873) is a sprawling attempt to wrangle the history of French food into a recognizable shape. It is an oversized book of 1,155 pages, filled with recipes, old stories, and new anecdotes by Dumas himself. It is charming and bewildering, and sacrifices accuracy for poetry. Dumas's entry on the truffle gives no factual information, but suggests its direct connection with the divine, and he informs us, erroneously, that the fifteenth-century French merchant Jacques Coeur brought the turkey back from Turkey. Dumas evidently recognized the blank space that was left in the history

ingenious tricks, and combinations lost? Some cookbooks in England, and, later, the United States, were written by women, though early on, of course, they were intended to be read only by rich women. Even this slight diversity of voices is likely to have played a role in England and America's comparative resistance to the hegemony of French cuisine. In 1651, François Pierre de la Varenne (1615–78) changed cookery forever with his *Le Cuisinier François* ('The french cook'), which laid the groundwork for every variety of haute cuisine. It is not a work of genius, though it is a very fine cookbook: it just happened to be the first work to integrate everything Europe had learned about cuisine during the Renaissance, whilst looking ahead to the Enlightenment. French cuisine overtook European high cuisine, giving the upper classes a common culinary vocabulary. The eighteenth century saw the first regional Italian cookbooks, a rush of great English

**ABOVE** | The frontispiece to Hannah Glasse's *The Art of Cookery, Made Plain and Easy... By a Lady* (c. 1775).

The caption reads:
'The Fair, *who's Wise and oft consults our* Book,
*And thence directions gives her Prudent Cook,*
*With* Choicest Viands, *has her Table Crown'd,*
*And* Health, *with* Frugal Ellegance *is found'.*

of food and tried to fill it, but he did so chiefly by repeating the sort of nonsense that had sprung up in the place of actual history – even if it was often rather diverting nonsense.

Soon, the blanks and counterintuitive facts drove me to research other rare books: histories such as Pliny's *Natural History* (first century C.E.), a compendium of classical knowledge that covers unicorns, Atlantis, and mayonnaise, and Bernal Díaz del Castillo's (1492–1585) *Historia verdadera de la conquista de la Nueva España* ('The true history of the conquest of new spain'), which mentions a recipe using the tomato over a century before it was included in the first cookbook. How could Pliny mention mayonnaise, when it was supposedly discovered by accident following the French victory at the Battle of Minorca in 1756?[1] Was the Seven Years War actually started by the French, to capture the Spanish recipe for mayonnaise?[2] Why is the turkey called a turkey, when it is from the Americas?[3] Why do the origin stories for the national dish (insofar as there is one) of Mexico, *mole poblano*, all take place after the arrival of the Spanish?[4] These are the sorts of questions to which I set out to find answers, and the answers, generally, were that food history was mostly made up.

All of this got me thinking that surely there was a way to fit food back into the historical narrative, some way to reconcile its place in our lives with its absence from written history? When we read a biography of, say, Napoleon, there is a certain pact made between reader and author that the historical events surrounding that great, short man all have some relationship to Napoleon himself. For the purposes of his story, and because he was of such vast and permeating importance, it is assumed that Napoleon's existence affected almost everything that

occurred in his lifetime. It doesn't even have to be said aloud. There is a dynamic between the shaper of history and history itself. Even Tolstoy's *War and Peace* (1869), which is in direct conflict with this idea that history is shaped by great individuals, somehow proves it by the void at its centre, where Napoleon surely lies: like a black hole, we can infer his presence from his absence. We enter a tacit agreement, when we read this sort of biography, that when the world moves, we feel that its subject had a hand in it. By elevating one figure above the events that enveloped them, we shift, however little, our entire view.

How can we raise food above its quotidian existence, without fancifying it beyond all meaning? As always, it is easy to talk about feasts for kings, and musky fruits washing up on far-flung shores, but harder to talk about real food. The first English cookbook, beloved of re-enactors and medievalists the world over, is a late-fourteenth century work that goes by the name *The Forme of Cury* ('The method of cooking', for 'cury' is from the ancient French verb *cuire*, meaning to cook). Written in Chaucer's lifetime, it is the first book I consulted when trying to recreate some of his food, but like almost all early cookbooks, it is a collection of recipes for royalty: in this case, it was put together by the chefs of King Richard II (1367–1400). Other early cookbooks are in much the same vein: the famous early-thirteenth-century French *Le Viandier de Taillevent* (loosely, 'The meat expert of taillevent') was written by a chef to the Vallis Kings; *Opera*, the marvellous Italian cookbook, was written by Bartolomeo Scappi, who traded upon his connection to the Vatican;

ANSWERS | [1] Because the French had decided to take credit for an early Spanish recipe. [2] Probably. [3] Thanks, Dumas. [4] Colonialism.

a fine early German cookbook was compiled by a cook to an elective prince of the Holy Roman Empire, and so the list goes on. Dinner, like history, was always made for the wealthy. My aim to elevate without aggrandizing, to bring food back to its deserved place in history, means that theories will have to leap across a few chasms of the unknown.

In the twenty-first century, we seem to be swimming in food: as evidenced by the proliferation of cookery television programmes, the slow-food movement, celebrity chefs, endless recipe books, cupcakes, the condemnation of gluten, et cetera. We spend our time not so much eating, as imagining that we are eating; not cooking, but contemplating cooking. We are less concerned or obsessed with food as we are enveloped by it, drowning in it. We are preoccupied by food in the same way that a hypochondriac is interested in their health: that is, obsessively and insatiably, because, after all, no matter how many epsiodes of how many cooking

shows we may watch, our bellies won't get any fuller.

History has misdirected our attention with wars, new discoveries, and horrors, like a magician making coins appear and disappear, so that, often at crucial moments, we have lost track of food. As if there was something unseemly about talking of the daily filling of our stomachs, the record has constantly been distracted elsewhere, only happy to return to the subject when armies' supply lines were cut, or when a famine descended. We are left to wonder what breakfast, lunch, and dinner might have consisted of when circumstances were not quite so pressing. The following chapters are full of food stories that, I hope, will start to fill in some of the empty and inaccurate spots in our history of food.

ABOVE LEFT | *The Forme of Cury* (1377–99).
ABOVE RIGHT | The frontispiece to Jules Gouffe's *The Royal Book of Pastry and Confectionary* (1874).

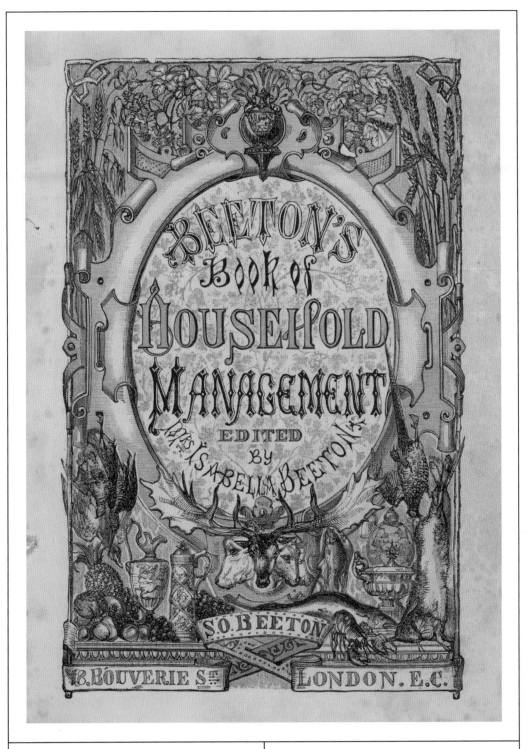

**ABOVE** | Mrs Isabella Beeton's *Beeton's Book of Household Management* (1859–61).

Though Mrs Beeton herself did not reach the age of thirty, her book held sway over English cookery for the better part of a century.

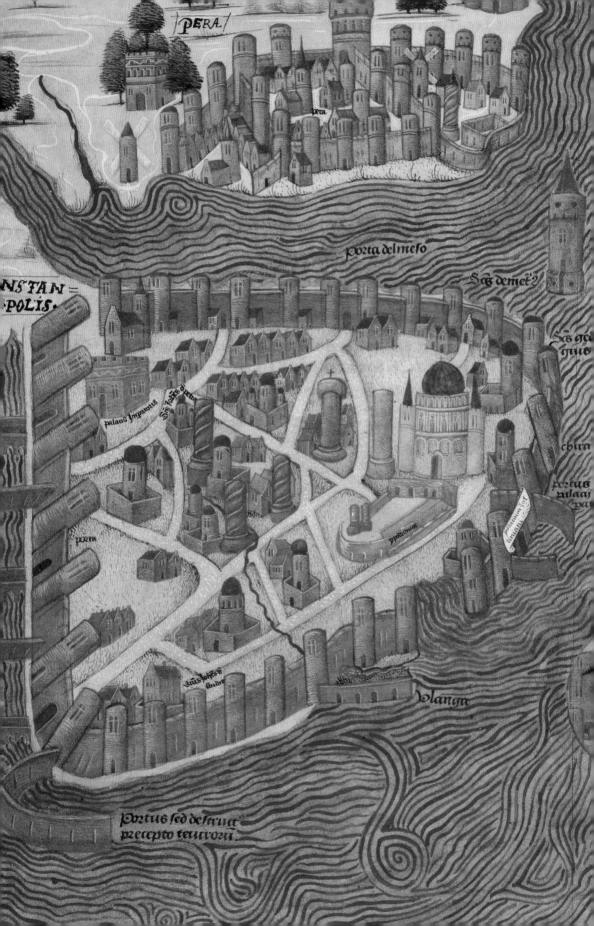

PERA

CONSTAN=POLIS.

Porta del meso

Scs demet

Scs greci nuus

palaciu Imperatoris

Scs Iohes dpeta

chira

portus palaci...

palaciu...

Yparonia

porta

saus Iohes d Andre

Ulanga

portus sed destruc precepto teutroru

# CHAPTER ONE

# CARP

## AND

## THE

# PEOPLE'S

# CRUSADES

With the collapse of the Roman Empire in the fifth century, the largely illiterate citizens of Europe fell into a long swoon and forgot much of what they once knew about art, architecture, indoor plumbing and even farming. Roman central government and trade networks withdrew, wars and recurring plagues took their toll, and urban populations scattered. The knowledge and skills that had been acquired under Roman rule withered away, so that Europe was actually left worse off than before occupation.

Among the developments that the Romans had introduced to Europe was the art of pisciculture – that is, the cultivation of fish in ponds and waterways, for food. A variety of farmed fish, especially pike and bream, contributed both much-needed

protein and welcome variety to the diets of ordinary Europeans. Pisciculture became widespread and made a large and steady impact on Roman citizens across the empire: fish were an easily harvested, high-quality food, as well as providing a tax income for local nobility. After the fall of Rome, fish farming slowly died out in the West – though this, art, architecture and indoor plumbing continued to be pursued in the East.

Some six centuries after the fall of Rome, in 1095 C.E., at the Council of Clermont in France, Pope Urban II called upon the Christian nations of the earth to take up arms and reclaim Jerusalem from the Muslims. He had recently received a letter requesting aid against hordes of invading Turks from the Byzantine Emperor Alexius, but the idea for the crusade had been gaining currency for several years. However, it would prove no mean feat to persuade thousands of poorly educated, ill-equipped, untrained and

OPENER | Constantinople, Christoforo Buondelmonti, *Liber insularum archipelagi* (1482). LEFT | St Anthony pictured with a victim of St Anthony's fire, from Hans von Gersdorf, *Feldbuch der Wundartzney* (1551). | ABOVE | Roman fish mosaic from the Villa dei Settimii (first century B.C.E.).

malnourished peasants to march across Asia to conquer a city they had never seen: one which had not, in fact, been Christian for some five hundred years, since the fall of Rome.

Earlier that year, the Hospital Brothers of St Anthony had founded a mission, confirmed by Pope Urban II, to treat the victims of ergot poisoning, then known as St Anthony's Fire. Ergotism was widespread in medieval Europe, and caused by ingesting grains infested with the *Claviceps purpurea* fungus, which displaces the grain's nutritious kernel. Symptoms of ergot poisoning include convulsions, headaches, vomiting, mania, as well as hallucinations, due to the lysergic acid it contains. An advanced symptom of ergotism is gangrene, related to the fungus's vasoconstrictive action. Medieval farmers did not know what the infestation was, so it grew year by year. Even today, it is not unheard of for ergot outbreaks to ruin ten per cent of wheat harvests. Peasants, who routinely ate and drank beer, soup, and bread as their main sources of sustenance, were teetering on the brink of starvation as it was, but the connection between the twin plagues of incipient madness and protein deficiency was not discovered until the late seventeenth century.

According to the anonymous author of *Gesta Francorum* ('The deeds of the Franks' *c.* 1100) Pope Urban II's speech evoked the 'illness, hunger, thirst, and other [ills]' assailing the European peasants. The Pope

ABOVE | A figure with symptoms of ergotism. Detail from Matthias Grunewald, *The Temptation of St. Anthony* (1510–15), Isenheim Altarpiece. | OVERLEAF LEFT A carp in Ibn Bakhtīshū, *Kitāb naʿt al-hayawān* ('Book on the characteristics of animals', 13th century), an Islamic bestiary. | OVERLEAF RIGHT | A spread Seder table from the Ashkenazi Hagadah (*c.* 1460).

attributed such atrocities to the Muslims as the rending of Christian flesh to expose riches that had been sewn beneath the skin, and inducing vomiting to access the contents of Christian stomachs. His intention was to blame Muslims for the starvation and madness that was stalking Europe in the form of ergot. Ironic, of course, because while most of Europe was still blundering through the Dark Ages, and still four hundred years away from inventing the table fork, the Muslim world was experiencing one of the greatest flowerings of science, mathematics, medicine, and engineering that the world has ever known. At the time, Muslims were much more likely to discover a cure for ergot than they were to be behind any of the ills affecting Europeans.

The Islamic world's practical science and medicine, as well as its (modestly) more egalitarian ideals, allowed for a better and more varied diet for its people. One innovation, likely left behind by the Romans, was pisciculture, and in particular the farming of carp: a prolific, fast-growing and omnivorous species

صُورَةُ الشَّبُّوط

الشَّبُّوط معتدلٌ من بين أصناف السَّمَكِ

مائِلٌ إلى الحرَارَةِ لِيُسرِعَةِ حَرَكَتِهِ وكثرةِ قَفَزَاتِهِ

مرَارَةُ الشَّبُّوطِ أنفع من سَائِر المَرَايِرِ وسُوِّي

لَحمُهُ الأَبدَان وَسِنفَعُ المَهزُولِ ولَبَن ع. واذا خُلِطَت

مرَارَتُهُ مَعَ مرَارَةِ ذِئبٍ وَأَمسَكَتها امرَاةٌ بِصُوفَةٍ

לַחְמָא עַנְיָא דִּי אֲכָלוּ אַבְהָתָנָא
בְּאַרְעָא דְמִצְרַיִם כָּל דִּכְפִין
יֵיתֵי וְיֵיכוֹל כָּל דִּצְרִיךְ יֵיתֵי
וְיִפְסַח הָשַׁתָּא הָכָא לְשָׁנָה
הַבָּאָה בְּאַרְעָא דְיִשְׂרָאֵל הָשַׁתָּא

leftover skin could then be stuffed to form the traditional Jewish dish known as *gefilte* fish, now much more commonly formed into balls or quenelles without the skin. Thus the carp's many bones became a feature, rather than a defect.) Carp spread prolifically in the Eastern world, resulting in a huge disparity in protein intake between East and West.

The first wave of crusaders is popularly known as the People's Crusade, although the 'Crusade of the Starving, Horrifying Mob' might be more accurate. It consisted of over 50,000 peasants, mostly poorly armed. They were led by a shoeless hermit named Peter, from Amiens, northern France, who was notable for subsisting entirely on fish and wine. The story goes that, on a previous visit to Constantinople a few years earlier, another great lover of fish, Jesus of Nazareth, had appeared to Peter in the Holy Sepulchre at Jerusalem and encouraged him to preach the crusade – and perhaps to bring the secret of carp farming back from the Holy Land as a sort of manna.

Energized by the fine sermons of Peter the Hermit and inspired by his vision of Christ, the People's Crusade wandered peacefully across Europe, via Hungary, and eventually arrived at the glittering city of Constantinople. Just kidding. They pillaged, robbed, murdered, and devoured their way across Europe in an orgy of violence, venality, and anti-Semitism: preying on the largely non-belligerent, defenceless Jewish population as a scapegoat for their new-found hatred of the Turks. If filling their bellies was what the crusaders were after, they should have stopped there. The Jewish people of Europe, forced by their fringe status to develop a parallel economy, had brought the secret of carp farming to Europe from Asia some centuries before. Had they noticed what the Jews were tending in

that had originally been domesticated in China. Carp can tolerate a wide variety of conditions, including weeks of being stuffed into a jug of water and fed table scraps, enabling the fish and its farmers to travel far and wide.

In the West, carp was unknown, except among the Ashkenazi Jews from Central and Eastern Europe. (Though carp is notoriously bony and the picking of bones is prohibited on the Jewish Sabbath, it was discovered that its many small bones are rich in gelatine which, when boiled, reduced and strained, form a delicious jelly called fish gelee. The

their backyard ponds, the Crusaders could have swiped a few carp, gone home, dug a pond, and eaten their fill in peace.

Instead, they continued their rampage, finally reaching the eastern limits of Christendom. There they beheld the riches and beauty of Constantinople, its fine churches and architecture stretched out before them. The French priest, Fulcher of Chartres, who was also a chronicler and advisor to the first King of Jerusalem, described the city thus when he arrived with the bulk of the troops:

*Oh, what an excellent and beautiful city! How many monasteries, and how many places there are in it, of wonderful work skillfully fashioned! How many marvellous works are to be seen in the streets and districts of the town! It is a great nuisance to recite what an opulence of all kinds of goods are found there; of gold, of silver, of many kinds of mantles, and of holy relics. In every season, merchants, in frequent sailings, bring to that place everything that a man might need.*

Faced with Constantinople's treasures, the Crusaders redoubled their efforts to rob, consume and befoul the city in paroxysms of unfettered gluttony. Emperor Alexius, seeing what a seething, uncontrollable mob his letters to Pope Urban II had unleashed, quickly commissioned boats to take them away from Constantinople and across the Bosphorus Strait, where they were to make camp and prepare for reinforcements before attacking Constantinople.

Introduced to ordinary life in

Turkish villages, the Christian hordes encountered – to their surprise – other Christians who, although they had been heavily taxed, had not otherwise been especially mistreated. They had been neither flayed alive for the silver secreted beneath their skin, nor forced to vomit the gold they had hidden in their stomachs, nor beaten and set aflame for their refusal to worship Allah. Strange. Having grown accustomed to causing mayhem, however, the Crusaders were undeterred, and pillaged Christians and Muslims alike. Peter the Hermit, though he himself ate only fish, encouraged elements of his group to cook and eat the fallen Turks, and to view them as 'new manna'. Thus the poorest and weakest of the Crusaders, unable to fight, could participate by consuming the enemy.

Peter the Hermit mysteriously wandered back to Constantinople for supplies just before the People's Crusade reached its sudden and ignominious end, at the Battle of Civetot, in 1096.

OPPOSITE | Carp and swallow woodblock print on paper, printed in Suzhou China, Qing dynasty (c. 1644–1753). | ABOVE | A tench, a roach, a burdot, and a carp. From an anonymous Flemish album of drawings (1637).

ABOVE | Knights on horseback, during the first Crusade. The miniature top left probably shows Peter the Hermit exhorting troops. Paolino Veneto, *Chronologia Magna* (c. 1323–50).

OVERLEAF | Fishing for carp in a pond, from Vincenzo Cervio, *Il Trinciante* (1593), an influential Renaissance text on carving, which also demonstrated how to use the newly popular fork.

Emboldened by false rumours, spread by the Sultan's spies, of the ample opportunities for pillaging and the certain victory that lay ahead, the Crusade wandered into a Turkish ambush and was destroyed. Peter escaped back to Amiens, no doubt with a few jugs of wine and carp and a burning ambition to launch a pisciculture operation in Europe. For the next two hundred years, waves of carp-fuelled soldiers raced to the Holy Land to fight, learn, wreak havoc, and, of course, to eat.

Back in Europe, carp rapidly became popular, and fish farming boomed. With the weekly demand created by the Catholic Church's prohibition from eating meat on Fridays and the difficulty of sourcing ocean fish inland, the hearty carp became a mainstay of menus for centuries. In fact, throughout the Middle Ages, it was a rare monastery, manor, or hamlet that didn't have their own well-stocked carp pond. Although it took slightly longer to cross the English Channel, by the time English cookbooks began to appear in the seventeenth century, carp had acquired its own pie.

Carp was everywhere, but was only a staple food for Jews, and those Central Europeans (the Poles, Czechs and Slovaks) who made it the centrepiece of their Christmas Eve feast. Though it was widely eaten in seventeenth-century England and the Netherlands, carp was not taken to colonies in Virginia, Massachusetts, or Quebec when Europeans settled in North America. In the early nineteenth century, it became apparent that the Americas were decidedly carp-deficient.

Carp arrived in North America in 1831, when Henry Robinson, owner of a transatlantic shipping route that began in Le Havre, released a few dozen French-born specimens in Newburgh in New York, though presumably not at the behest of Jesus Christ. Le Havre, as it happens, is the closest major port to Amiens, and it is not beyond the realms of possibility that the bloodlines of these fish could be traced back to the time of Peter the Hermit. Though the great American showman P.T. Barnum himself tried to take credit for bringing the carp to America, most scholars agree that it is Robinson's carp that made their way into the Hudson River when his ponds overflowed in a storm.

The original carp immigrants brought over by Robinson are named the mirror, leather and common carp. At the time of writing, there is a well-publicized fear of carp taking over the public waterways of the United States, especially the Great Lakes. Most of the talk converges on new 'Asian carp' that are apparently spreading unchecked, edging out local fish and destroying vegetation. One species in particular, the silver carp, has a dangerous but picturesque tendency to leap into the air when startled by motorboats. Conveniently forgotten is the fact that *all* carp are Asian carp and that these recent species, escapees who were imported to control algal growth in fish farms, are just the latest members of the carp family to have made the trans-oceanic trek.

The spread of carp across the United States was interrupted, first by the Mexican–American war (1846–8), and then by the American Civil War (1861–5). The country may have been pieced back together, but its agriculture was a mess. Southerners in particular were relying too heavily on corn for their primary protein, which led to pellagra, a nutritional deficiency disease that caused symptoms, including dermatitis, diarrhoea, and dementia, not unlike those of ergotism. Fields were ruined and families torn apart. Despite the cessation of hostilities, there

remained a mutual distrust between North and South.

In the 1870s, with no less an aim than uniting the divided nation through a shared love of carp, the United States government began importing the fish, mostly from Germany (many still refer to them as 'German carp'), and building vast state-run fish farms. By the end of the decade, the government had initiated an annual carp lottery and was distributing tens of thousands of fish to all parts of the country (in 1883 alone, 298 of 301 districts were provided with over 260,000 carp). Contemporary fishery reports cite a 'fever of enthusiasm' for carp culture, and the lotteries were always oversubscribed. Pleased to be able to put their differences behind them and, then as now, enthusiasts of anything offered for free, the citizens of the United States were eager to get their hands on as many fish as possible. Carp were planted in ponds, canals, ditches, swamps, rivers (including the Mississippi), and lakes – they especially thrived in Lake Eerie – as well as in state fish farms. Carp propaganda issued by government leaflets

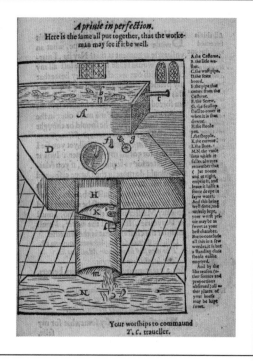

TOP | Fishing for the Common Carp in a river. Gottlieb Tobias Wilhelm, Discourses on Natural History (1812). | ABOVE | An attempt to describe a machine for fish farming, in Sir John Harrington's *A new discourse of a stale subject, called the metamorphosis of Ajax* (1596). | OPPOSITE | A recipe for carp pie in Robert May, *The Accomplisht Cook* (1671).

*To bake a Carp according to these Forms to be eaten hot.*

Take a carp, scale it, and scrape off the slime, bone it, and cut it into dice-work, the milt being parboild, cut it into the same form, then have some great oysters parboild and cut in the same form also ; put to it some grapes, goosberries, or barberries, the bottoms of artichocks boild the yolks of hard eggs in quarters, boild sparagus cut an inch long, and some pistaches, season all the foresaid things together with pepper, nutmegs, and salt, fill the pyes, close them up, and bake them, being baked, liquor them with butter, white-wine, and some blood of the carp, boil them together, or beaten butter with juyce of oranges.

*To bake a Carp with Eels to be eaten cold.*

Take four large carps, scale them and wipe off the slime clean, bone them, and cut each side into two pieces of e-very carp, then have four large fresh water eels, fat ones,
boned

stressed the ease and joy of carp farming, and the unmatched fertility of the fish, while relegating what, precisely, to do with all your carp to the small print. It was considered enough just to *own* carp. The excitement that swirls around goldfish contests at county fairs, where children timorously toss ping-pong balls into goldfish bowls for the right to take one home, is a vestige of the carp fever that once gripped the United States.

For all the success of the breeding program, carp failed to take hold in the kitchens of the United States, and carp recipes in nineteenth-century North American cookbooks are few and far between. Even cookbooks catering for the humble table, and featuring catfish, turbot, and eels, fail to mention the common, but difficult to prepare, carp. English recipe books were frequently imported, but also seldom featured carp, and typically relied upon French or German recipes. Actual English recipes, still common in early-nineteenth-century cookbooks, generally ceased to be included in English cookbooks until around the mid-twentieth century, though Mrs Beeton persisted with a robust carp section in her *Book of Household Management*. Beyond Jewish and Chinese immigrants, with whom they remained enormously popular, carp never gained much traction as a foodstuff in the States. Omnivorous, enormously fertile, hardy, and often regarded as inedible, it is no wonder that wild carp spread so very quickly. In 1937, scientists discovered the simple chemical cure for pellagra in the form of vitamin B3, or niacin, and by the early twentieth century, the fashion for carp slowly ground to a halt. Carp, not realizing that they had fallen out of favour, swam on, popular only with fringe sport fisherman for their bulk, and the difficulty of coaxing them onto a line.

The United States government also sent large numbers of carp to Ecuador, Costa Rica, and Mexico (where they continue to thrive), as well as west to California. From California, carp were sent to Hawaii, where they found approval with Chinese and Japanese settlers. These were the same populations of settlers that had already brought their own 'German' carp from Asia around a hundred years earlier, thereby assisting the fish in completing a millennial circling around the globe, and meeting their long-lost relatives in the scenic irrigation ditches of Wailuku.

OPPOSITE & ABOVE | New York State Hatching House in Caledonia, New York. Robert Barnwell Roosevelt and Seth Green, *Fish Hatching and Fish Catching* (1879). | OVERLEAF | *Two Carp* (1831). Woodcut by Katsushika Hokusai.

*La Belle Limonadière*

CHAPTER TWO

# LEMONADE

# AND THE

# PLAGUE

In 1668, the bubonic plague, which had been dormant for a decade, had returned to France and was threatening the population of Paris. It had been reported in Normandy and Picardy: in Soissons, Amiens, and then, terrifyingly, just downstream of the capital along the Seine, in Rouen. Everyone knew what this meant. Only a few years previously, between 1665 and 1666, London had lost over 100,000 people to the plague – almost a quarter of the population. Many still remembered 1630, when the disease had killed nearly a third of Venice's 140,000 inhabitants, and almost half of Milan's 130,000. Panic-stricken Parisian public health officials imposed quarantines and embargoes in the hope of mitigating inevitable disaster – but the dreaded pestilence never struck.

The plague that loomed over Paris was the midpoint of a seventeenth-century European epidemic that would go on to decimate Vienna (80,000 in 1679), Prague (80,000 in 1681) and Malta (11,000 in 1675). The body count in Amiens would end up topping 30,000, and almost no city in France was spared – except for Paris, which, miraculously, survived almost completely unscathed. Typically, the more important a city – and thus the greater the traffic, movement, and population density – the greater the risk of disease, and the faster it spreads. How is it possible that the capital city of France, one of the most visited and populous cities in Europe, escaped virtually intact from a plague that devastated much of the continent?

Lemonade has been called the world's first soft drink. It was passed down to the Egyptians from prehistory, and slowly spread over the globe, making summertime just a little more pleasant. Its citric acid helped to prevent bacterial growth in drinking water, meaning that

lemonade drinkers were marginally more likely to survive. In the early twenty-first century, it has become fashionable to drink lemon slices in hot water to aid digestion, 'detoxify', and help maintain a slightly alkaline body pH – but for a few months in 1668, I contend that lemons conferred far greater benefits. That summer, lemonade kept tens of thousands of Parisians from joining the victims, in London, Vienna, and Milan, of Europe's last Great Plague.

Ever since the late 1650s, Italians and their visitors have been treated to a huge range of soft, hard and mixed drinks, available both in cafes and from street vendors. Among those drinks on offer are eaux de vie and a variety of neutral spirits with infusions such as cinnamon, anise, angelica, raspberry, amber and musk, apricot, and currant; spiced wines such as Louis XIV's favourite, *hypocras*; non-alcoholic drinks such as the almond-

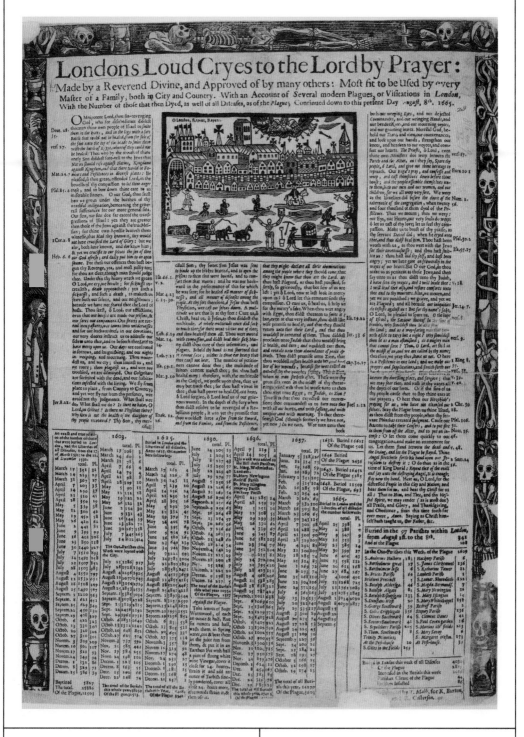

**OPENER** | *La Belle Limonadiere,* hand coloured etching (1816). | **OPPOSITE** | Plague in 1665. Etching and engraving by James Hulett (c. 1740–71).

**ABOVE** | London's Loud Cryes to the Lord by Prayer: Made by a Reverend Divine... (c. 1665). **OVERLEAF** | Map of Paris by Jan Ziarnko (1616).

VIL L

porte st anthom

fides

La Place
Dauphine

Cheual de
Bronze

A PARIS c
Anthoine de Vuarcon
au pallais en la galler
prisonniere. ANNO

English two years after publication and remained in print for over a century. A recipe that used both lemon and orange peel had also appeared in *Le parfait confiturier* ('The perfect jam-maker', 1667, usually attributed to La Varenne). Shortly before his death, Cardinal Mazarin – who liked nothing better than new things he could tax – brought limonadiers to Paris. World-class megalomaniac that he may have been, even Mazarin could not have guessed that lemonade might have saved so many lives, in a few short years.

and-rosewater tonic *orgeat*; and, of course, lemonade, and its pulpier compatriot, *aigre de cedre*, a mixture of lemon juice, pulp, zest, sugar, and water. Cost, and the limited geographical scope of suitable farmland, had held lemonade back, but when hardier, juicier varieties of lemon were cultivated and trade routes sped up, its price came down, and its popularity skyrocketed. As befits its delicious and refreshing simplicity, soon everyone in Rome wanted lemonade on a sultry summer's day, and vendors began to carry tanks of it around the city.

Parisian visitors to Italy – such as Cardinal Mazarin (1602–61), who had succeeded the diabolical Cardinal Richelieu (1585–1642) as chief minister to the King of France – left wondering why they didn't have limonadiers carrying fresh beverages around their own fair city. Lemonade was already being drunk in Paris: it had appeared in François Pierre La Varenne's groundbreaking *Le Cuisinier François*, a cookbook so popular and influential that it was translated into

OPPOSITE | Limon ponzinus chalcedonius, from Giovanni Battista Ferrari's *Hesperides sive de Malorum Aureorum* (1646), the first major botanical work on fruit. | ABOVE LEFT | Orangery and lemon trees recorded in Jan van der Groen, *Le jardinier du Pays-Bas* (1672). | ABOVE | Italian street seller of lemons. Etching after Annibale Carracci (1646).

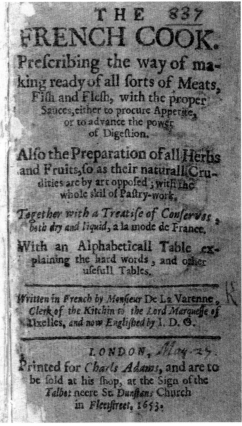

The bubonic plague that was spreading through Europe is generally believed to have been transmitted by flea bites. Many now believe that fleas infected with *Yersinia pestis* plague bacteria were transported aboard gerbils, themselves incidental passengers on ships from the Far East. When these gerbils arrived in Europe, their fleas spread to the extensive and ubiquitous European rat population. Fleas carrying the plague virus were distributed around cities by rats, switching from rats to humans or domesticated animals as their rat host succumbed to plague, and back to other rats as they killed their human hosts. Rats could just as easily blame humans for transmitting the fleas back to the rat population and, for all we know, they do.

The key to this method of transmission is how intimately urban rats and humans live with each other: everywhere people create organic refuse, so go rats. Despite the devastation associated with the bubonic plague, it is actually a surprisingly fragile construct that leads to its spread through a metropolis. Each element in the chain – flea, rat, human – has to be set up perfectly for the plague bacterium to cause an epidemic, or it will fizzle out. This is thought to be why, thankfully, the plague only struck every few hundred years, rather than constantly cycling through Europe – and it also explains why it was disrupted in Paris, in 1668.

The Parisian fad for Italian-style beverages was cresting throughout the late 1660s and early 1670s – so much so that, in 1676, Louis XIV reached an agreement with the vendors to combine the lemonade business with that of the French distillers, mustard-grinders and vinegar-makers who had been squeezed by the French monarchy in 1394: forming the *Vinaigriers moutardiers sauciers distillateurs en eau-de-vie et esprit-de-vin buffetiers*. While the name could have used some brainstorming, this was in fact the world's first corporation. The alliance was more fitting than they knew, because for centuries it was vinegar that took pride of place as the most effective plague repellent.

By the seventeenth century, the mechanisms of person-to-person transmission of the plague were beginning to be understood. While it took centuries to discover the role that vermin played,

precautions of varied effectiveness were taken to prevent the spread from infected humans. Doctors, apparently more concerned with their health than bedside manner, wore black robes, and long-beaked, bird-like masks filled or impregnated with vinegar and herbs to counter airborne pathogens. A group of burglars, taking advantage of general disorder and empty houses, used a

OPPOSITE TOP | Frontispiece and titlepage, Francois Pierre de la Varenne, *The French Cook* (1653). OPPOSITE BOTTOM | Frontispiece to *Traité de Confiture; ou le nouveau et parfait confiturier* (1667).

ABOVE | The famous plague doctor costume of the seventeenth century. The long 'beak' contained herbs and vinegars thought to protect against miasmas. Watercolour, c. 1910. | OVERLEAF | Microscopically enlarged flea in Robert Hooke, *Micrographia* (1665).

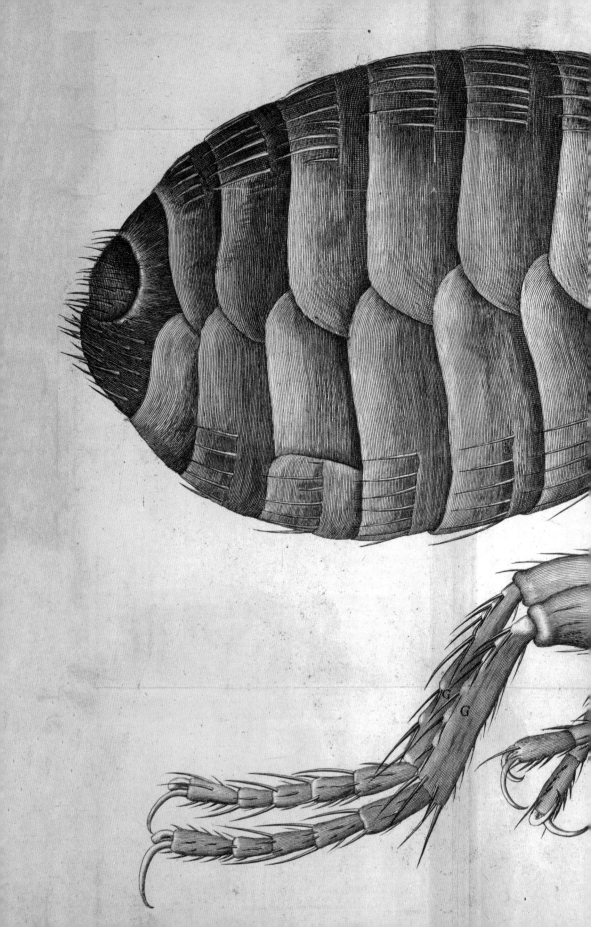

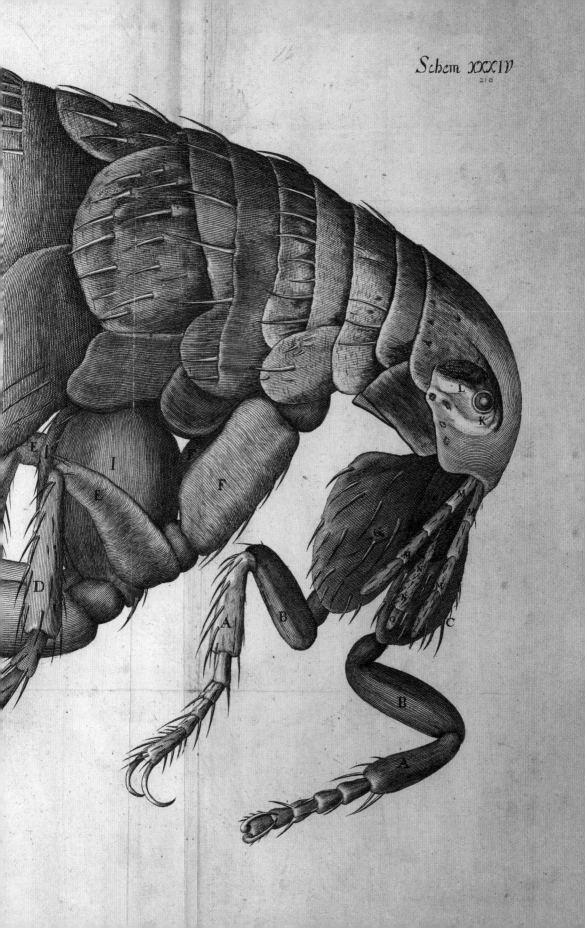

PER AVER
MULTIPLICATO LA
PESTE
CON UNGUENTI

QUI DOVE ESISTE QUESTA PIAZZA
SORGEVA UNA VOLTA TONSTRINA
A GIO. GIACOMO MORA
IL QUALE FATTA CON GUGLIELMO PIAZZA
PUBBLICO COMMISSARIO DI SANITA'
E CON ALTRI UNA COSPIRAZIONE
CON MORTALI UNGUENTI QUA E LA DISPERSI
MANDO' MOLTI A CRUDA MORTE
GIUDICATI PERTANTO AMBIDUE NEMICI DELLA PATRIA
SOPRA ALTO CARRO
TENAGLIATI PRIMA CON ROVENTE MORSA
E PRIVATI DELLA MANO DESTRA
COMANDO' IL SENATO
DI FRANGERLI COLLA RUOTA
E NELLA MEDES. INTRECIATE DOPO SEI ORE DI SCANNARLI
QUINDI DI ABBRUCIARLI
ED ONDE NIENTE RIMANGA DI SI SCELERATA GENTE
III GETTARE LE CENERI NEL FIUME
E CONFISCATI BENI
DALLA QUAL COSA ONDE SIA LA MEMORIA ETERNA
COMANDO' DI DISTRUGGERE
QUESTA CASA OFFICINA DI TANTA SCELLERAGGINE
E DI NON MAI POSTERIORMENTE RIEDIFICARLA
ERRIGGENDO UNA COLLONA
CHE SI CHIAMI INFAME
LUNGI DA QUI LUNGI PERTANTO
CITTADINI BUONI
ONDEL INFELICE INFAME SUOLO
NON VI CONTAMUNI
ANN. MDCXXX.I. AGOSTO

| ESSAVO PUB. PRESID. | PRESID. DEL SENATO | R. JUSTITIAE |
| MANT. MONZIO SENATOR | GIO. BATTA. TROTTO | CAPITOMS BAPTISTAE |
| | | VICE COMITAR |

COLLONA

INFAME

FRENCH-LEMONADE-MERCHANT.

Pub.ᵈ accord.ᵍ to Act of Parlt.ᵗ June 1ᵗ by X Scratchley 1771.

saliva or picking up infected fleas, it did little to address the greater issue. No, I propose that what derailed the spread of the plague into Paris in the summer of 1668 was lemons.

The Parisian lemonade fad took hold so quickly that the business was likely still to have been in the hands of the street vendors when the plague surrounded the city. Lemonade was not only popular, but ubiquitous, and carried by limonadiers into every profitable corner of the city. The limonene contained in lemons (and other citrus fruits) is a natural insecticide and insect repellent. The most effective part of the lemon is the limonene-rich peel. Indeed, after centuries of discovery of chemical insect repellents, the United States Environmental Protection Agency lists fifteen insecticides in which limonene is the chief active ingredient, including both general bug sprays and products for pet flea and tick control. The French were piling lemon peels and the crushed husks of lemons used for *aigre de cedre* into the best possible place to disrupt the flea-rat-human-rat chain: the trash. In this way, the city was effectively, if accidentally, covered by limonene: limonadiers patrolled the more affluent areas, and the cast-off peels and husks took care of the poorer districts. The rats would not only have been unbothered by the huge quantities of lemon, but, being omnivorous, probably quite happy to try this new flavour. Serendipitously, fleas infected with plague bacteria would have been killed.

Many of the other recently introduced beverages also had insect-repellent

concoction that came to be called *vinaigre des quatre voleurs*, or 'vinegar of the four thieves'. This mixture of herbs, garlic, and vinegar was both imbibed and sprayed or daubed around the mouth and nose, to prevent the inhalation of noxious 'miasmas'. It has actually proven a sound and convenient recipe for a general pest repellent, and was reproduced in cookery and medical books well into the twentieth century. If vinegar of the four thieves had been sprayed far and wide, maybe cities other than Paris would also have escaped the plague.

What such remedies failed to target was the precise vector: it was the fleas, rather than the rats, or noxious fumes, which were the central problem. Though being doused in vinegar of the four thieves and having worn a plague-doctor mask would indeed have helped to protect an individual from person-to-person transmission of the plague via close contact with bacteria-laden

PREVIOUS | The torture and execution of alleged plague carriers in Milan, 1630. | ABOVE | A caricature of a French lemonade merchant, after Henry William Bunbury (1771). | OPPOSITE | Satire of an eldely man buying a glass of lemonade from a street vendor (1814).

LE NOUVELLISTE EN DÉPENSE

*Déposé à la Direction de la Librairie &c.*

properties: the anise of eau d'anise, juniper in esprit de genièvre, coriander in eau de coriandre, fennel in eau de fenouil, and the list continues. Indeed, a number of the most commonly used herbs in the imported drinks were themselves ingredients in vinegar of the four thieves. In Paris, in 1668, almost nowhere would have been safe for a plague-carrying flea. It would not have been possible for fleas to survive in the general refuse or in sewers, normally good places to find rats, as they would have been loaded with limonene and other repellents. Millions of desiccated fleas must have pined for those gerbils as they died in the streets, while the rats and humans enjoyed their good fortune.

In the years that followed, all sorts of people tried to take credit for saving Paris from the recurrence of the bubonic plague. Gabriel Nicolas de la Reynie, appointed the first Lieutenant General of the Police of Paris in 1667, built his burgeoning reputation for progressive law enforcement on peacekeeping and preventing the plague from taking root. Ministers such as Jean-Baptiste Colbert, who pushed through trade restrictions requiring the careful airing of goods before they were brought into Paris, along with the six major guilds and the magistrate Jacques Belin, applauded themselves for their foresight. The royal counsellors who watched them do it hired people to slap them on the back for their staunch support, and Louis XIV (1638–1715) celebrated by annexing several more Belgian towns from the Spanish. But one of these days, someone in Paris will come to their senses and erect a bronze statue of a limonadier, staring boldly ahead while casting a used-up lemon over their shoulder into a pile of rubbish. Maybe it will even bear the legend: *Les rats, désolé, nous toujours avons pensé qu'il était vous* ('Sorry, rats, we always thought it was you').

SIROP DE

CITRON

PUR SUCRE

IMP. M. MARIAGE PARIS          N° 131 M          MOD. DÉPOSÉ

OPPOSITE | *La Nécessaire Herboriste* (1827–9). Note the large jar of lemons alongside the leaves and herbs that make up her trade. | ABOVE | French lemonade advert from the late nineteenth century.

OVERLEAF | Lithograph advertising iced lemonade in New York, *c.* 1879.

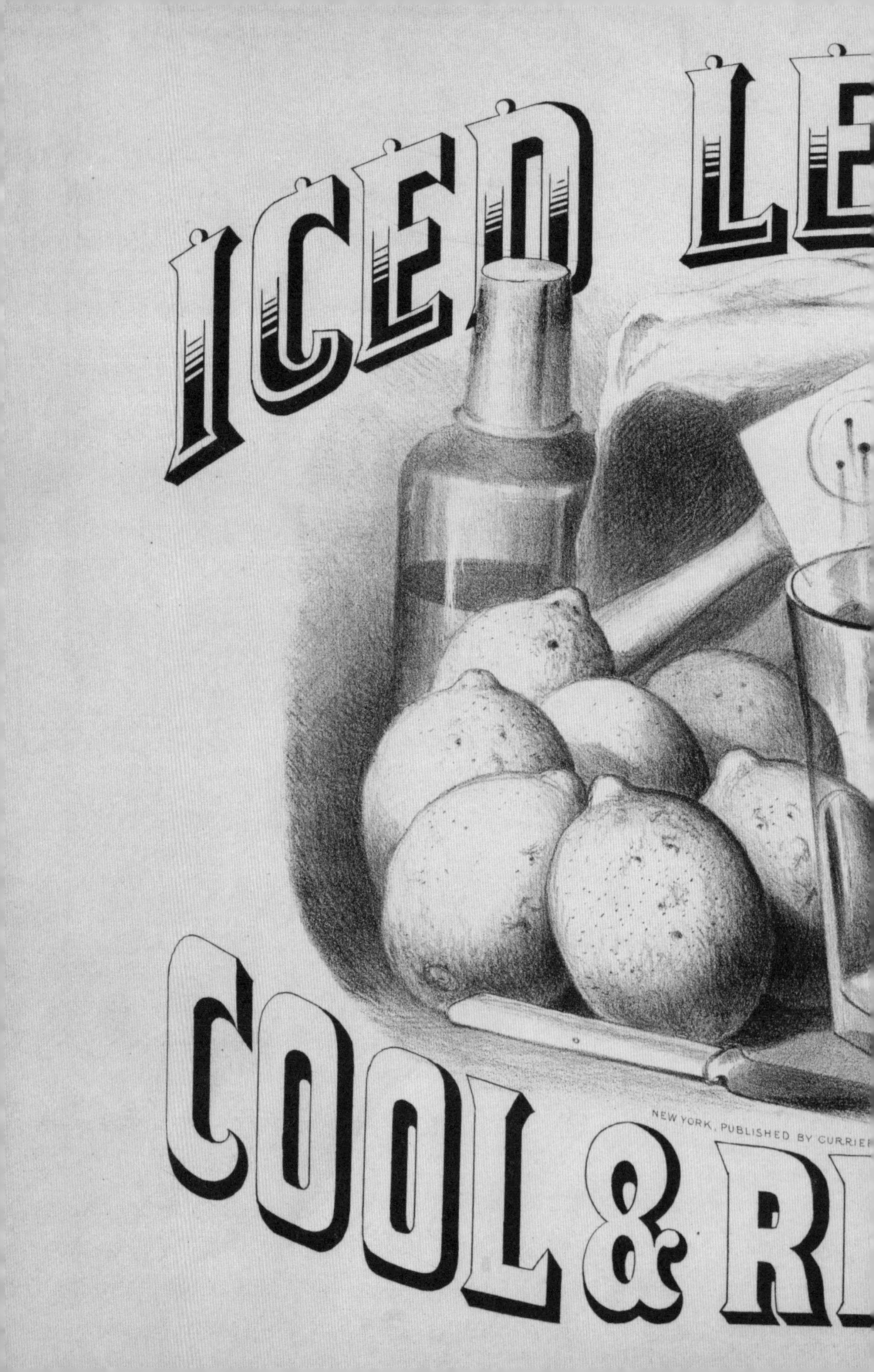
ICED
COOL &
NEW YORK, PUBLISHED BY CURRIER

MONADE

FRESHING

SSAU ST.  COPYRIGHT, 1879

# CHAPTER THREE

# EXTRACT

## *Abstraction*

It all started because people, particularly armies and navies, wanted to carry around huge quantities of soup without, you know, carrying around huge quantities of soup. Sometime around the mid-to-late seventeenth century, people began to dehydrate soup stock into cakes that were convenient to transport and rehydrate. At least, they began to do it commonly enough that it appears in the written record: it was one of those ideas that was sufficiently obvious that people had probably been dabbling with it for quite some time. However, because it was time-consuming, expensive, and tricky to bring the reduced soup to cohere into cakes that could be rehydrated, recipes were slow to catch on. By 1733, when Vincent La Chapelle wrote *The Modern Cook* (published in French, in 1735, as *Le Cuisinier Moderne*), despite having been knocked around for at least fifty years, the recipe was still certifiably insane:

*The Way of making Broth-Cakes, which may be conveniently carried Abroad, and preserved above a Year.*

Take a quarter of a large Bullock, a whole Calf... two Sheep, and two dozen of old Hens or Cocks or a dozen of Turkeys pick'd, drawn, and squashed with the Calf, and put them all into a large Copper with the Calf's feet and Sheep trotters scalded and clean'd...

Add to the decoction twelve or fifteen pounds of Hartshorn Shavings, which must be boil'd apart and strained off whilst hot.

Then pour over the whole four pail-fulls of spring water; cover the Copper close; stop it round with some Paste, put sixteen pound weight upon it boil it without skimming, on slow fire, for six hours or more, till the whole be sufficiently boil'd, which is known by the Bones coming off easily:

Then take out the large Bones, leaving the rest a stewing; and when done enough, take out your meat quickly, and mince it immediately; then put it in a large hot press, cover'd with Iron, to squeeze out all the Gravy:

This done, pour the extracted Gravy into the Copper, where the Broth remained, and presently strain the whole together through a hair Sieve to take away the filthiness; then let it cool, and take off the fat: Season this Broth immediately, with a moderate quantity of Salt, pounded white Pepper, and Cloves; set it on to boil again, stir it continually till it turns to brown Jelly (when pour'd into plate) as thick as Honey. Then take it off, let it be half cold; then pour it directly into some glazed earthen Vessels which are long and flat, and not exceeding three inches in depth. As soon as it is quite cold, let it be dry'd, either in a hot Copper Oven, or in another Oven; after the Bread is taken out, take care your Broth does not burn or parch. It must be as stiff as Glue, so that it may be easily broken with your hands, and make your Cakes of it, each weighing an ounce or two, which you must keep in glass Bottles in a Box or Barrel well clos'd in a cool and dry place, to be used when occasion requires. These cakes, when dissolved, are very relishing, and may be used either for ordinary Broth or Soops.

BOUILLON OXO EN FLACONS
**CHIMISTES CELEBRES.**
5) Le laboratoire de J. v. Liebig à Giessen (1840).

Reproduction interdite.                    Voir l'explication au verso.

Soup-making was revitalized at the turn of the nineteenth century, when the inventor Sir Benjamin Thompson (1753–1814), known as Count Rumford – an Anglo-American Loyalist version of his contemporary Benjamin Franklin (1706–90) – found that while the German army was just as poorly supplied with rations as any other, they savoured their soup in such a way that made them happier and healthier. He cleverly recognized that this feeling of well-being was more than the sum of the pleasure of consuming the soup plus its nutritional value. Rumford invented a very simple soup, made of pearl barley, split peas, potatoes, bread, salt and vinegar, which gestures at this interaction of soup and mind. When cooked slowly, these ingredients produce molecular flavour precursors that mimic the flavours of heartier, meat-based soups, and produce the feelings of satiety that Rumford admired.

Though there were incremental improvements in the development of portable soup (not least those made around 1831 by the father of canning himself, Nicholas Appert), there were no substantial changes in either theory or process until the Liebig Company launched a massive operation out of South America in 1865. Baron Justus von Liebig (1803–73) was an eminent German chemist whose name endures because he lent both it and his theories to the

OPENER | Bovril Supports the World, advertising poster, c. 1885. | ABOVE | Liebig trading card, showing Justus von Liebig and his laboratory. The Liebig company created thousands of trading cards to publicize their product. Each set consisted of six cards grouped around a partcular theme.

OVERLEAF | Four sets of Liebig trade cards. From left to right: the length of the Rhine, Non-European straits, European straits, and rivers in France. Late 19th century.

Liebig Extract of Meat Company. In one of his books, *Chemical Letters* (1843), Liebig speculated that the South American cattle industry, which generally only raised cattle for their hides, could be leveraged to produce huge quantities of meat extract to be sold into the European market, bring meaty nutrition to those too poor to afford British beef. A few enterprising souls read this, obtained financial backing, and convinced Liebig to join just such a scheme. They started with 28,000 head of cattle on the Uruguay River at Fray Bentos, and built a factory to process the huge quantities of beef that were reduced in the proportion of thirty kilograms of cow to one kilogram of meat extract. The process, though industrialized, was not noticeably less crazy than La Chapelle's recipe from 130 years before, but the scale was monstrous.

The notion of meat extract is similar to the French technique for making *glace de viande*, reducing meat stock to a concentrated paste. However, as is often the case, industrialization added speed, efficiency, and a heaped dollop of something quite revolting. Much like the notorious plants that fermented and liquefied huge piles of fish to produce the Ancient Roman fish sauce known as *garum*, nobody wanted to go near the Liebig plant with their olfactory faculties intact. But, unlike the *garum*-processing method (which involved macerating the fish in salt, and curing the mixture in the warmth of the sun for at least a month, until the sauce was formed), the Liebig factory used enormous steel rollers to smash the beef into a pulp, which was boiled, steamed, rendered, and reduced to a thick, brown gravy. The resulting gloop was then bottled and shipped to England, with excessive promises of its nutritional value predicated on that thirty-to-one ratio.

Initially, Liebig's Extract of Meat was sufficiently popular that such temptingly named products as Johnston's Fluid Beef (1870) and Liebig's Extract of Meat and Malt Wine (1881) were launched onto an unsuspecting world. They were later renamed Bovril and Wincarnis, respectively, and still enjoy a surprising and somewhat disturbing popularity. Bovril remains in demand both as a condiment and as a hot beverage (try it with hot milk for a taste of the whole cow). It is a portmanteau word made up of 'bovine' (Latin, *bovem*) and the name of the advanced species from Edward Bulwer-Lytton's book *The Coming Race* (1871), who derive their vast powers from a mysterious electromagnetic substance called 'vril'. Really, in the late-nineteenth century all you had to do was rub a little science on a product and *boom*! The railroad, the telegraph, and Bovril: welcome to the future. Even more so than the absurd, and absurdly profitable, Liebig Extract of Meat and Wine company (which, by the way, was in large part responsible for giving birth to the great deforesting beast that is the South American cattle industry), Bovril seems representative of this moment in time when science seemed not just effective, but magically, inevitably, capable of fixing *everything*.

Once scientists started probing the nutritional benefits of Liebig's Extract of Meat, it turned out that all that smashing and pulping, boiling and rendering, cooking, and squeezing, did away with many of the nutrients in the original beef. The company then, to

OPPOSITE | Stickers created to advertise Johnston's Fluid Beef, *c.* 1885. | OVERLEAF | Cattle on the March to Fray Bentos, the Works of the Liebig Extract of Meat Company, in South America. From *The Illustrated Sporting and Dramatic News*, 25 January 1890.

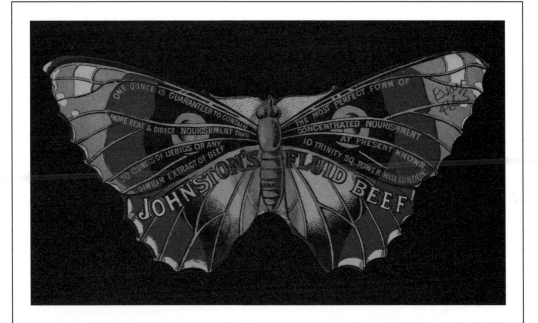

use current business parlance, pivoted, and re-marketed the extract to middle-class households as a comfort food. You might not have expected this to work. A product that from its inception was designed to concentrate the nutritional value of large quantities of beef into a convenient jar that was portable and affordable for soldiers, the impoverished, and people who simply needed to inject massive quantities of beef into their bodies without all that inconvenient meat and gristle, but actually ended up being of little nutritional value and too expensive for most of its intended market, should have been an utter failure – but it

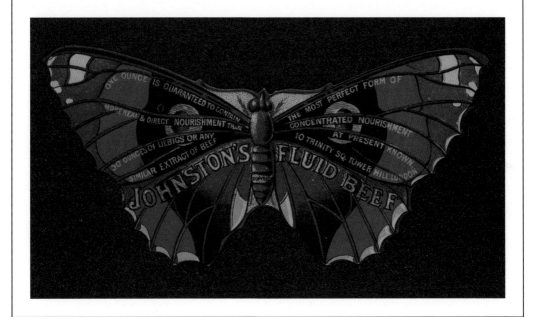

CATTLE ON THE MARCH TO FRAY BENTOS, TH
IN SO

S OF THE LIEBIG EXTRACT OF MEAT COMPANY,
MERICA.

wasn't. The middle class gobbled up the newly reconceptualized meat extract as if completely unaware that it hadn't been intended for them all along – and maybe, in a funny way, it really was.

In 1902, another Liebig discovery – that yeast cells could be exploded and eaten – burst on to the market. The discovery was a natural one: when it had become clear that the attraction of Liebig Extract of Meat was not the nutrition, or even the taste, but a quality that seemed quite ineffable, the famous chemist went searching for that ineffability and found it inside yeast cells. In fact, the original name of Marmite might have been 'Liebig's Ineffable Viscera of Yeast', had it not been named instead after the rotund earthenware casserole dish that contained it, and which its glass jar still imitates. When yeast cells explode, they release all

of their amino acids, including glutamic acid, which, in addition to signalling to your brain that it is eating protein, is a neurotransmitter. These signals are what provide the flavour that many describe as 'savouriness', when tasting certain foods. Though most of the goodness was lost from the beef in conversion to Liebig Meat Extract, the glutamic acid remained to impart the sensation that one was consuming all that cow – a sensation that could be rather more cheaply and simply imparted by freeing the glutamic acid inside of yeast cells.

Soon after its invention, Marmite

ABOVE | Bovril advert from 1886. | OPPOSITE
A particularly bloodthirsty advert for Lemco,
a type of meat extract manufactured by Liebig.
From *The Graphic*, 1904

was included in every First World War soldier's rations, to supply them with B vitamins and a positive attitude. As the mechanism of this taste became clear (the glutamic acid inside the yeast cell becomes liberated when the cell is autolyzed by salt, which causes the yeast cells to shrivel up and explode, and then bonds with salt to form monosodium glutamate, producing the weirdly savoury and satisfying flavour that made Liebig's Extract of Meat popular in the first place), companies began substituting some of the beef in Bovril, Wincarnis and similar products with autolyzed yeast. It turned out that consumers either couldn't tell the difference, or actually preferred the yeast version. For a few years after the British beef export ban in 2004, Bovril was made with no beef at all. Since the ban was lifted, it is once again made with a mix of yeast extract and beef stock, though there is little evidence that anyone can tell the difference.

In 1907, a few years post-Marmite (P.M.), Japanese researcher Kikunae Ikeda – grasping after what made the simple preserved skipjack tuna (known as *katsuobushi*) and *kombu* kelp Japanese broth *dashi* so deliciously comforting in a way that was not explainable by the four known tastes (sweet, salty, bitter, sour) – would isolate monosodium glutamate. He called this fifth flavour 'umami', meaning 'pleasant, savoury taste'. Like Rumford, Ikeda was hoping to elevate the lives of the rural poor by making their food more pleasurable without the cost of meat, and, like Liebig, the appeal was to the blossoming value of science as a general, enlightened, good. Monosodium glutamate, or MSG, is formed, simply speaking, when free glutamates meet salt, or another source of sodium molecules. The glutamates are naturally present in the kelp that is boiled to make the broth, just as chemically and gustatorily significant quantities are naturally present in foods such as meat, anchovies, tomatoes, mushrooms, Parmesan, and

**I WANT PROTECTION!**

They take me from my home afar,
Where all my noble brothers are,
And put me in a little jar,
And call me **LEMCO.**

blue cheeses. Quickly realizing that they were on to a good thing, MSG was branded *Aji-no-moto* ('The essence of taste') and commercialized, in 1909. It quickly penetrated the Japanese market, and a shaker of *Aji-no-moto* could be found on almost every Japanese table, not just those of the rural poor. As questions about its health effects began to leak in from the West in the late 1960s, the shaker became less prevalent, but the flavour continues to animate Japanese food.

Monosodium glutamate was never seriously marketed with a brand name for Western tables (though there have been a few half-hearted roll-outs, such as Accent in the United States). Instead, food companies introduced it as an additive and sold it into restaurants, particularly Chinese ones. Following in the steps of Liebig's Meat Extract, it found immediate and lasting success inside comfort foods of negligible nutritional value: the aforementioned

Chinese fast food, snack chips, and, of course, canned soups, stews and chowders. True to its roots in portable soup, MSG also featured prominently in field rations. During the Allied occupation of Japan (1945–52) following the Second World War, leaders noticed that their soldiers preferred to eat Japanese rations, rather than their own, whenever possible. When MSG was found to be the source of this disparity, it was swiftly added to the rations of the United States army. In fact, until recently, MSG was a compulsory additive in United States army rations – Count Rumford would have been so pleased.

ABOVE LEFT | Oxo, *The Tatler*, 30 November 1928.
ABOVE | Oxo, *Britannia & Eve*, December 1929.
OPPOSITE RIGHT | Oxo, *The Sphere*, 2 November 1912 | FAR RIGHT | Bovril, *Pan*, 8 November 1919.
OVERLEAF LEFT | Marmite advertising poster, 1929.
OVERLEAF RIGHT | Bovril advertising poster, 1890.

Quite well Doctor, thanks to you and
OXO

BOVRIL

A "Little Bovril"
keeps the Doctor away

As the twentieth century progressed, real beef products went through a tough time. Interest in healthier foods conspired with stagnant economies, chicken's greater popularity, and stocks of canned foods full of meat-simulating MSG flavour, to blunt beef's appeal. It was increasingly clear that glutamate and cow were engaged in a zero-sum game. This flavour, born in England by way of South America, from a thousand smashed cows, like Bovril before it, betrayed its beefy past. By the 1960s, MSG was lending its magical sensation to so many pre-packaged and canned foods, especially in the United States, that the beef industry felt compelled to respond. Around 1968, reports of headaches, sweating, palpitations, facial numbness, nausea, and weakness began to appear. Whether the beef industry was directly responsible for the avalanche of anecdotal evidence relating to MSG's side effects, or they only benefited from them,

is hard to discern. What we do know is that contemporaneous with these health reports was a push by the beef industry to modernize their marketing message and lobbying programme. Regional and national beef organizations, some in existence for almost a century, began to join together to fight the MSG threat. In 1973, they convinced the current President of the United States, Richard Nixon (1913–94), to freeze beef prices in order to appeal to an increasingly squeezed population in the grips of 'stagflation'. The freeze was a catastrophic mistake, tanking beef prices and allowing MSG, though its reputation had been tarnished, to continue to placate unruly populations well into the 1980s. The reprieve was short, and complaints of 'Chinese-Restaurant Syndrome', a catch-all term for a variety of ailments linked by convention and repetition to MSG, spelled doom for monosodium glutamate. It was forced underground and disappeared

MARMITE
MARMITE
for Health and Good Cooking
Carried Unanimously
WOOLLEY

BOVRIL
BOVRIL
30, FARRINGDON ST., E.C.

UNWIN BROTHERS, LITH LONDON, E.C. (COPYRIGHT)

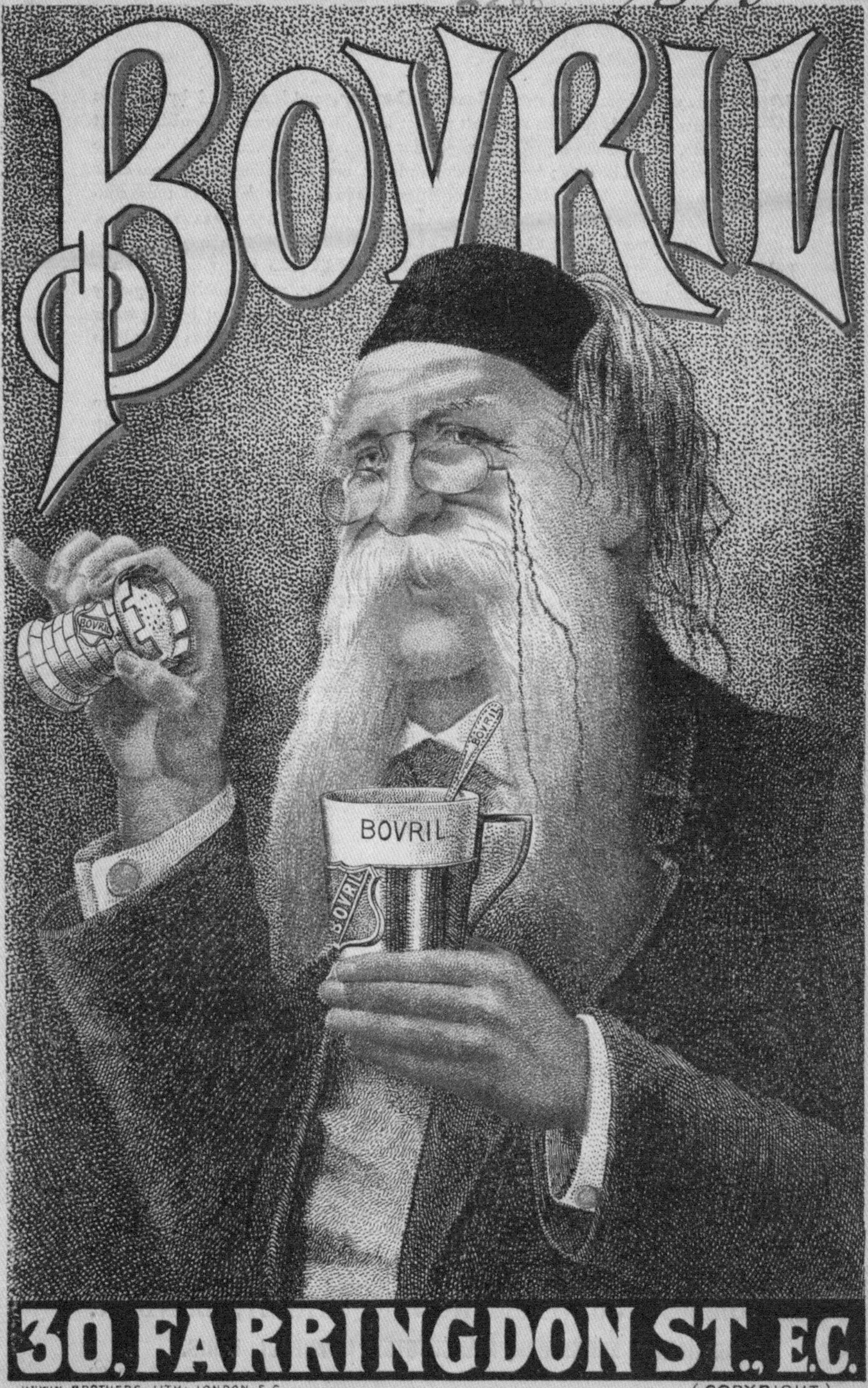

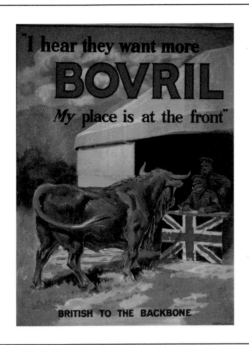

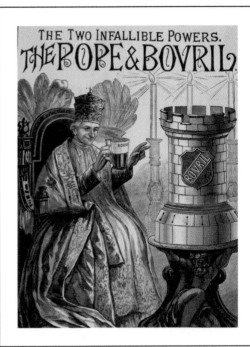

from food labels to be replaced by its precursors, such as autolyzed yeast and hydrolyzed protein, both of which contain glutamic acid that turns into MSG in the presence of salt, but are not treated as such from a food-labelling standpoint.

Why have vegetarian groups never come strongly to the rescue of MSG? At least in the spirit of 'the enemy of my giant cow-shaped enemy is my friend', they should have been on the same side, after all. It seems like the 1970s or 1980s would have been a perfect time for them to plunge into the fray as East and West, seaweed and cow, kelp soup and barley soup all sought a decisive victory. But vegetarians have always been tepid at best on the suspiciously chemical-sounding MSG, and the food-additive label with which it was lumbered. Later, its alleged side effects seem to have kept from adopting it those who might otherwise have been pleased to sprinkle MSG on their tofurkey, or to use it instead of salt (MSG makes small quantities of salt taste saltier). So the moment of rapprochement

passed vegetarians by, and we marched into a new millennium with no resolution in sight, as MSG and its ever-dwindling allies do battle with cows everywhere.

Recently, attempts to recast MSG as an idea rather than a substance have seen some success. Umami has been severed from the chemical as surely as Bovril was severed from the cow, and now roams free to make meals dance with the essence of taste. Once again, of course, it's not the poor folks eating Rumford's soup who carry a torch for umami, but the middle (and even upper) class. It turns out that, even after all this time, it is still easier to sell comfort and satiety to the comfortable and sated. The poor, as usual, will have to fend for themselves.

ABOVE LEFT | Bovril in WWI. Poster, 1915. | ABOVE The Pope & Bovril. *Illustrated Sporting and Dramatic News*, 1 March 1890. | OPPOSITE | Bovril will make a man of him. *Pan*, 15 November 1919. | OVERLEAF LEFT Liebig trade card, 1890. | OVERLEAF RIGHT Aji-No-Moto. Mid-20th century poster.

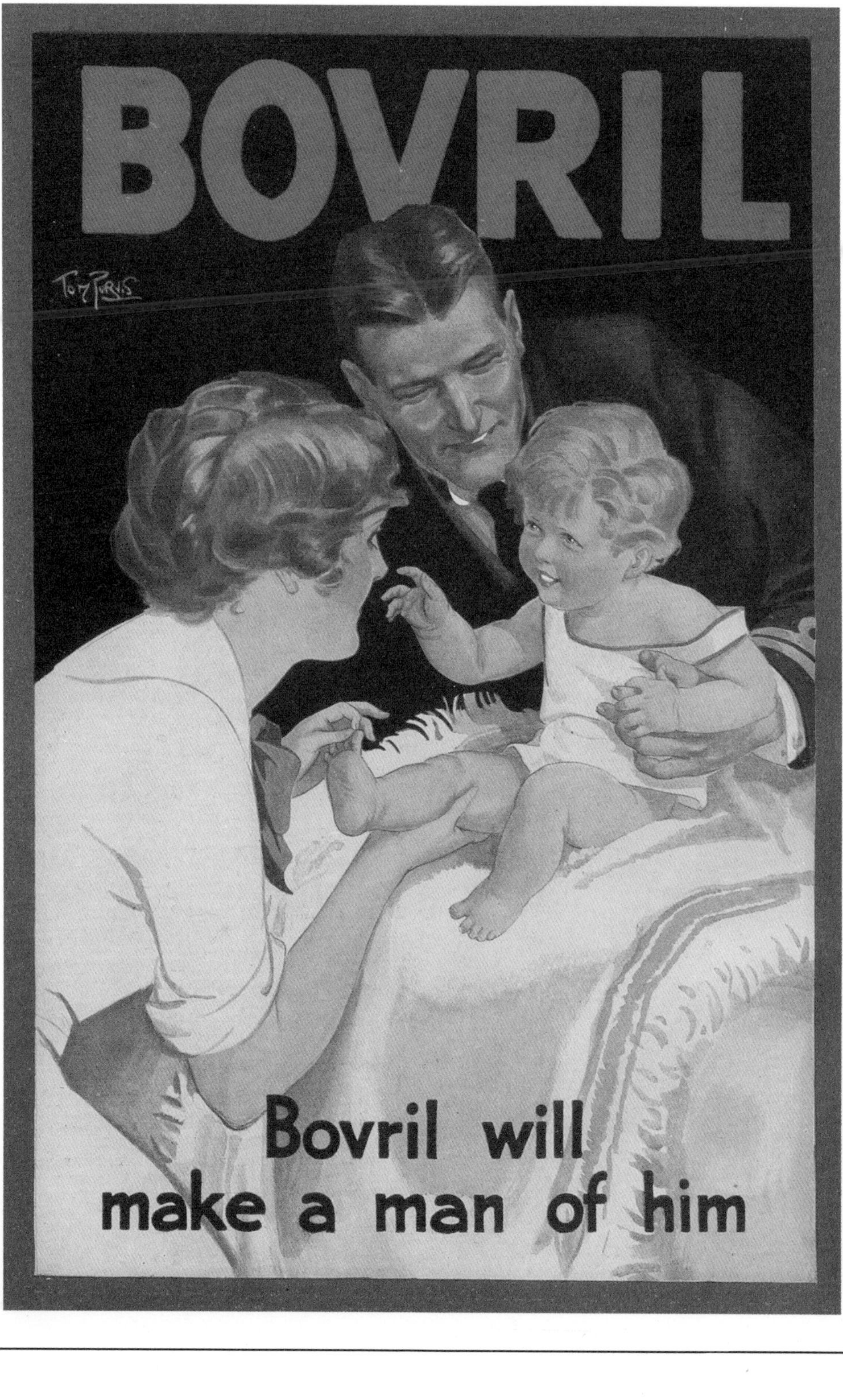
BOVRIL
TOM PURVIS
Bovril will
make a man of him

# AJI-NO-MOTO
## ESSENCE OF TASTE

調味精粉

味の素

Hic sunt
antropo
phagi

# CHAPTER FOUR

# EVERYBODY

# E A T S

# SOMEBODY,

# SOMETIMES

Everybody eats somebody, sometimes. It's just a question of the circumstances: plane crashed, boat capsized, lost in the woods, just defeated a hated enemy in battle, zombie apocalypse.... Europeans have been obsessed with what constitutes 'acceptable' cannibalism for centuries: so much so that the 'six people in a boat but only enough food for four' scenario is a staple of ethics classes the world over. No less an authority than the Catholic Church has proclaimed that cannibalism to prevent starvation is acceptable, as long as you don't actually kill anyone, or pray for 'that delicious-looking vegetarian to die first'. Non-industrial societies have often taken a more sanguine view, and chosen to eat only people 'over the mountain'. The reasoning is that if they eat only 'others', it doesn't seem so much like cannibalism: it's more like a tiger eating a lion.

That said, non-European cultures often have even more emphatic taboos against cannibalism, such as the monstrous arboreal beast created by a cannibal act: the ever-ravenous, never-sated Wendigo, of North American native, Algonquian, mythology. In general, though, the more people there are around, the more cannibalism is proscribed, at least notionally. Cannibalism in cities is more dangerous than in rural areas, because there are more people to eat, and their more varied diet makes them potentially more delicious. The social contract is sundered so completely when we size up our neighbours for dinner that it then becomes extremely difficult to, for example, borrow someone's lawn mower. These proscriptions can cause their own set of problems, as some people then fetishize the idea – taken over, like a child whose parents have hidden the cookie jar, by just how delicious a food must be to be so utterly *verboten*.

The word cannibal comes from the Carib, the indigenous people of the Lesser Antilles who also gave us the name of the Caribbean and – perhaps

not coincidentally – barbecue. The most famous early record of cannibals is Hans Staden's report from Brazil on the Tupinambá people. Published in German in 1557, it is entitled the *True Story and Description of a Country of Wild, Naked, Grim, Man-eating People in the New World, America*, which, at least, is descriptive. Staden's book has the Tupinambá eating people with some regularity: mostly roasted, but occasionally boiled for more domestic occasions. Their practices form the backbone of the theory of the great French anthropologist Claude Lévi-Strauss:

namely, that cannibals roast people they want to destroy and boil those they want to cherish – fire for your enemies, water for your family. The Tupinambá also made an entrail stew for the women and children that sounds similar to *menudo* (a spicy Mexican soup made from tripe), or the Filipino blood stew *dinuguan*, and which they called *mingau* (amusingly, now the name of an American beef jerky company).

Interestingly, one of the great city-based civilizations is also one of the most famous for cannibalism. By the turn of the sixteenth century, in a rare collision of

OPENER & OPPOSITE | Detail of cannibals on the Andaman Islands, from Ptolemy's *Geography* (1522). ABOVE Detail of *cynocephaly* (dog-headed people) practising cannibalism, from Ptolemy's *Geography* (1522).

OVERLEAF | Scenes of Tupinambá cooking and eating humans, from Theodor de Bry, *America* (1590). These engravings are based on the descriptions by Hans Staden in his book *True Story and Description of a Country of Wild, Naked, Grim, Man-eating People in the New World, America* (1557).

tem subigunt, Mingau vocatam, quam illæ adhibitis liberis absorbent. Lact
comedunt, tum carnes circa caput derodunt. Cerebrum, lingua, & quicqu

esui est in capite, pueris cedit. Finitis hisce ritibus, singuli domum repetunt,
sumpta portione sua. Auctor cædis aliud adhuc nomen sibi imponit. Regu
tugurii brachiorum musculos supernos scalpit dente cuiusdam animantis
cisori: vbi vulnus consolidatum est, relinquitur vestigium, quod honori mag
ducitur. Quo die cædes perpetrata est, auctor eius se quieti dare necesse hab
& in lecto suo retiformi decumbere totum eum diem: præbetur illi arcus n
ita magnus, cum sagitta, quibus tempus fallit, & scopum ex cera adornatum
tit. Quod fit, ne brachia ex terrore cædis obtusa, seu exterrita fiant tremula
sagittando. Hisce omnibus ego spectator, & testis oculatus interfui.

Numeros non vltra quinarium norunt: si res numerandæ quinarium
cedant, indicat eas digitis pedum & manuum pro numero demostratis. Que

si n

Americani defixis in terra ligneis quatuor furcis crassitudine brachii, trium
edum interuallo, quadrata figura, æquali vero trium fere pedum altitudine,

aculos in transuersum duobus à se inuicem distantes digitis superimponunt, **Boucan es**
aque ligneam cratem comparant: hanc sua lingua *Boucan* nominant. In ædi- **Barbaro-**
us permultas huiusmodi crates habent, quibus carnes in frusta concisas impo- **rum culi-**
unt, & lento igne siccis è lignis excitato, vt ferè nullus existat fumus, quamdiu **na.**
ert volutas coqui hunc in modum patiuntur singulis dimidiæ horæ quadrã- **Conseruan**
us inuersas. Et quoniam sale cibos minime cõdiunt, quemadmodum hîc mos **dorum ci-**
st, vno tantum coquendi remedio vtuntur ad eorum conseruationem, itaque **borũ apud**
tiamsi 30. vno die feras quales hoc capite describemus, essent venati, omnes **Americ.**
custatim concisas illis cratibus ingererent, quam citissime fieri posset, ne cor- **ratio.**
umperentur: ibi sæpius circumactæ aliquando plus quatuor & viginti horis
orrentur, donec pars interior carnium æque cocta sit atque exterior, eaque ra-
ione omnes sint à corruptione tutæ. Nec in piscibus apparandis & cõseruan-

circumstances that practically necessitated the eating of people, the Aztec Empire had grown to a size and density wherein its ability to feed its citizens was stretched to the very limit. As the Aztec did not domesticate herbivores of any kind – no cows, pigs, sheep, goats, or even guinea pigs – most people living in Tenochtitlán and Tlatelolco (in what is now Mexico) almost exclusively subsisted on corn, in a perpetual state of near-starvation. Given a precariously balanced urban population with a completely unbalanced diet, a rigidly hierarchical society, angry gods to appease and a citizenry inadvertently

OPPOSITE | Titlepage from Bernal Díaz del Castillo, *Historia verdadera de la conquista de la Nueva España* (1632 edition). | ABOVE | Cannibalism scene from Codex Magliabecchi (*c.* 1529–53). From facsimile of 1903. OVERLEAF | Cannibalism and human sacrifice in the Codex Borbonicus (c. 1507–22). From facsimile of 1899.

rendered delicious by their corn-based diet, there was a certain inevitability that the rich would begin to eat the poor. Like the Tupínambá, they also developed a recipe for their cannibal cookery.

Spanish conquistador Bernal Díaz del Castillo's (1492–1585) memoir of fighting to overthrow the Aztec Empire in Mexico with Hernán Cortés (1485–1547) – *Historia verdadera de la conquista de la Nueva España* ('The true history of the conquest of new Spain', *c.* 1578) – records what is apparently the standard recipe for stewing people with 'salt, peppers and tomatoes'. In addition to being the best contemporary recipe for human flesh, it is also the first recorded chilli-containing recipe and, by more than a hundred years, the first recorded tomato-containing recipe (tomatoes did not become popular in Europe until the end of the seventeenth century. Incidentally, Castillo suggests that chilli did not originally include

beans, settling the age-old chilli-con-carne argument). Very recent research on Aztec human bones found near Mexico City, which were stained red and yellow by spices, corroborate Castillo's recipe. The traces of stew examined by researchers also contained pumpkin seeds, chillies and possibly annatto (an orange-red carotenoid dye and mild spice from the seeds of the achiote tree), suggesting that people could have been an ingredient in early *mole* dishes, as well. All of which makes sense from a gustatory point of view, as the acidic tomatoes would cut through the reported sweetness of cooked human flesh.

Polynesia became famous in the eighteenth and nineteenth centuries for cannibalism, and their (questionably translated) terminology is the source of the famous 'long-pig' name for cooked people. In turn, usage of the term 'long-pig' is responsible for the widespread idea that people taste like swine – a fact that I can neither confirm nor deny. Most European accounts of cannibalism were thinly veiled attempts to justify the much more horrible acts with which they were engaged – as the French essayist and philosopher Michel de Montaigne (1533–92) so rightly noted (see below). For their part, the cannibal stories with which native populations regaled Europeans were meant to titillate, awe, and terrify, and were themselves wildly exaggerated. In many cases, each side told cannibal tales that alternately nullified and magnified the other's, which resulted in blurry reports of questionable veracity.

The Maori of New Zealand and Fijians definitely ate people (see Paul Moon, *This Horrid Practice*, 2008), and they also seem to have also followed Lévi-Strauss's theory that we roast our enemies and boil our friends. However, for all their fame as people-eaters, Polynesians are not strong on recipes, not even in the silly stories they told eager invaders. In fact, in the whole history of cannibal cultures, the Aztec and Tupinambá are the only ones to have left us a recipe more advanced than, say, the Fijians' 'long-pig with herbs.'

15.

los 6 aqui naciom ou
dicos y despuy

This would suggest that most of the other cannibals that Europeans obsessed over – the Arawak, Iroquois, Fijians, and so on – were engaged in relatively isolated, ritualistic cannibalism, the meaning of which was opaque to European observers. Without some spice and a sauce or two, even the most flavoursome people eventually get to taste monotonous.

Ever since the late sixteenth century, these reports appear to have stoked a European and, later, North American, mania for the idea of cannibalism. Europeans have routinely tried to pin cannibalism on the cultures they were disrupting and subjugating, using it to imply basic savagery and an absence of civilization. In nineteenth-century North America, psychologists began diagnosing Algonquin people with 'Wendigo psychosis', a supposed disease that manifested itself as a strong urge to eat people, even in the presence of other food choices. But a funny thing happened on the way to branding these civilizations with the scarlet 'c': much of the modern Western world became obsessed with cannibalism.

There exists a great literature of cannibalism, remarkable for its size, given that this is supposed to be one of the greatest taboos of Western civilization. Much of it, while interesting, is not really about eating people. Jonathan Swift's *Modest Proposal* (1729) that the wealthy English eat Irish children, and Michel de Montaigne's progressive and eminently sensible *Of Cannibals* (1580), in which he compares the depredations of Europeans to the relatively inoffensive habit of cannibalism, are both political rather than culinary in nature. The Ancient Greek Stoics Chrysippus and Zeno thought cannibalism was probably acceptable, but there is little to suggest that they put aside their philosophy and picked up

their forks. Authors Gustave Flaubert (1821–81), Herman Melville (1819–91), and Daniel Defoe (1660–1731) all wrote about cannibalism, but with little in the way of specifics. The great Mexican muralist, Diego Rivera (1886–1957), claimed to have lived, with a few friends, as a cannibal for two months, 'and everyone's health improved.' Rivera allegedly sourced his meals from the morgue, only eating those 'who had been freshly killed and were not diseased or senile.' He stopped 'not out of a squeamishness, but because of the hostility with which society looks upon the practice.'

The most famous cannibal in literature and popular culture is, of course, Doctor Hannibal Lecter, the notorious serial killer of Thomas Harris's novels, introduced in *Red Dragon* (1981). Lecter, though, is more of a cautionary tale against cannibalism: a manifestation of a nightmare, wearing an ascot, and listening to Brahms. The notion of a well-educated, highly cultured, aesthete, obsessed with eating people in the style of *nouvelle cuisine*, is an interesting psychological flight, but as cannibalism it is nonsense. Like Hannibal Lecter, most famous real-world cannibals aren't really proper cannibals at all, but crazy people. The twentieth century saw a smorgasbord of cannibalism presented at the cinema. The movies *How Tasty Was My Little Frenchman* (a 1971 retelling of Hans Staden's notorious report from Brazil, *sans* Staden), two accidental-cannibalism classics, *Eating Raoul* (1982), and *The Cook, the Thief, His Wife and Her Lover* (1989), as well as a bevy of others, continued the West's mixture of revulsion and obsession with cannibalism, with no hint of a resolution.

One of the only places where you can detect any real development of cannibal cookery is in English literature. From many of the plays of William Shakespeare (1564–1616) to the Victorian children's story

'Jack and the Beanstalk' (1807) and much by Charles Dickens (1812–70), English authors have been obsessed with the concealing of human flesh in food. In *Titus Andronicus* (1594), two characters are baked in a pie and served to the unsuspecting; Jack's giant grinds people's bones to make his bread; the popular penny dreadful story 'String of Pearls' (1846–47, later called 'Sweeney Todd', and an attempt to portray the Irish as cannibals just as much as it is a traditional horror story) portrays a murderous barber selling his victims to a pie shop; and in *Martin Chuzzlewit* (1843–4), a few years before the appearance of 'Sweeney Todd', Dickens makes mention of people baked in pastries. Dickens, in fact, repeatedly alludes, both obviously and subtly, to cannibalism in his works. Pip is threatened with being eaten in *Great Expectations* (1861); Fat Boy suggests he'd like to eat Mary in *The Pickwick Papers* (1836); cannibal and people-eating ogre references run through *A Tale of Two Cities*

(1859); and David in *David Copperfield* (1859) frequently makes reference to Dora in cannibalistic terms. But all of these are just appetizers placed daintily before the main course. In 1868, Dickens wrote a series of food pieces, the last of which, entitled 'An *Entremet* of Great Merit' detailed a few recipes from a 'cookery-book the property of the last chef of the King of the Sandwich Islands'. The recipes include 'the English sailor à la maitre d'hôtel', 'baby à la Metternich', scalloped ship-boys, and breadcrumbed captain with plum sauce. Dickens even explains that cannibalism is just a case of a craving for animal foods when all the indigenous creatures have been eaten: the subtext being, of course,

ABOVE | Human sacrifice at the great morai at Attahouroo, Tahiti, witnessed by Captain Cook on 1 September 1777. From *Drawings executed by John Webber during the Third Voyage of Captain Cook, 1777–1779.*

Beating the Death Drum for a Cannibal Feast

that the savage cannibal is free to chow down in public for lack of other options, but the English cannibal must disguise the victim of his appetite.

These references are so pervasive that I would suggest that Dickens was himself suffering from a peculiarly English type of Wendigo psychosis, in which the sufferer wants to eat human meat but only if it is hidden, like vegetables in a child's meal, and they themselves are protected from awareness of eating it at the time. Which really makes a lot of sense. We have been drawn and repulsed by the idea of eating

people for so many centuries, pinning our wicked dreams on other groups of people so that we could simultaneously revile and live vicariously through them, that this is the only logical method of resolution. Am I suggesting that Dickens and, perhaps, a cross section of nineteenth-century Englishmen were eating people pie and bone bread, to satisfy an urge that they could not admit to themselves? I would not go that far. However, I might take a look at how many orphans went missing in Charles Dickens's neighbourhood, just to be certain.

ABOVE LEFT | 'A Brazilian' depicted in Johannes Nieuhof, 'Voyages and Travels into Brazil and the East Indies', in Churchill, *A Collection of Voyages and Travels* (1732). | ABOVE RIGHT | 'Beating the Death Drum for a Cannibal Feast'. An exotic postcard produced in London, *c.* 1913 to satisfy the desire for cannibals.

OPPOSITE | George Dibdin Pitt, *Sweeney Todd, the Barber of Fleet Street; or the String of pearls. A legendary drama, in two acts, etc.* (1883). | OVERLEAF | *The Lamentable and Tragical History of Titus Andronicus... A ballad* (*c.* 1660).

# DICKS' STANDARD PLAYS.

# SWEENEY TODD,

## BY GEORGE DIBDIN PITT.

## ORIGINAL COMPLETE EDITION.—PRICE ONE PENNY.

**\*\*\* THIS PLAY CAN BE PERFORMED WITHOUT RISK OF INFRINGING ANY RIGHTS.**

LONDON: JOHN DICKS, 313, STRAND.

# THE

# CHAPTER FIVE

# DINNER

# PARTY

# REVOLUTION

In medieval Europe, upper-class meals were traditionally served with all the dishes presented at once, in a style now known as *service en confusion*. Those invited to eat were compelled to dote upon lord and lady, and to be doted upon in turn by those beneath them. Everyone behaved as befitted their station, so that even at a large gathering or festival, no beheadings were deemed necessary. Knives and hands were the only implements, and food was eaten out of pastry crusts or from hard, thick slabs of bread known as trenchers. While a normal dinner might consist of just a few people (and in winter, when food was scarce, possibly just the lord), elaborate feasts were held in spring and summer with three or four lavish courses consisting of random dishes served in succession. Because of pilferage, re-use and waste, it is difficult to reconstruct the exact size of these gatherings from the descriptions, but they were certainly rowdy affairs that required a full complement of cooks, servants, and specialists (such as clergy, to say the benediction, and poison testers, bearing magical utensils, for royal feasts). Kitchens at this time were barely controlled conflagrations, typically kept at some remove from the dining area and often housed in a separate building, meaning that a slow, guarded procession of dishes needed to be taken to the dinner table, which must have resulted in some rather tepid meals.

After the adoption of individual plates and forks for eating (rather than those that already existed for cooking and serving), around the early sixteenth century, meals became a little fancier, but didn't change much in tone. Then the French king Louis XIV (1638–1715) established the decadent Renaissance equivalent of the feudal dining system. Following the revolutionary movement known as the Fronde, that erupted between 1648 and 1653 within the emerging French middle class, Louis XIV had decided to keep a close eye on the nobility and to offer those who could afford it an opportunity

OPENER | Honoré Daumier, *Camille Desmoulins in the Palais Royal Gardens* (1848–9). | OPPOSITE | Two men eating, from *Flore de virtu e di costumi* (c. 1425–50). ABOVE | A peacock pie, from Christoph Weigel, *Abbildung der gemein-nützlichen Haupt-Stände...* (1693).

OVERLEAF | The Dukes of York, Gloucester, and Ireland dine with King Richard II. From Jean de Wavrin, *Anciennes et nouvelles chroniques d'Angleterre* (late fifteenth century).

Er parle dune grant feſt

to advance themselves in his good graces by moving to Versailles. Some estimate that as many as ten thousand members of the highest nobility were brought to live at the palace. They were required to witness the entrance of the king's dinner, and to watch as he and his family feasted on the twenty or thirty dishes, *au public*, which typically constituted the royal evening meal. Some five hundred people staffed the kitchen for these elaborate banquets, which lasted precisely forty-five minutes, from 10 to 10.45 p.m. During the meal, nobles were forbidden from making dinner conversation, eyes at prospective mistresses, or even exchanging glances when the king would pack away veal sweetbreads stuffed with ham on top of the partridge potage, seafood bisque, duck with oysters, scallops, chestnut soup with truffles, grilled pigeon *à la Sainte-Menhout*, pâté en croûte and seven other dishes he had sampled even before the *entremets* had

arrived. The king had cleverly found a way both to continue the medieval tradition of pomp, ceremony, and devotion that he felt was suitable for *le Roi du Soleil*, and remove such hindrances as having to eat with, or listen to, others. It also allowed him to enjoy the recent advances in French cuisine – the first great French cookbook, *Le Cuisinier François*, had been published ten years before Louis XIV's coronation – that had set his country apart from all others of Europe at the time. Louis Quatorze was simply highlighting his power and centrality, but a few dinner parties I have attended could have benefited from his rule of silence, not to mention his forty-five-minute decree.

Being the cunning glutton that he was, Louis XIV also no doubt believed that the fad for small dinner parties would prevent large groups of dissatisfied subjects from gathering together and discussing how to kill him – which it possibly did. Over

several decades, the fashion for small dinners percolated through French society and became the norm. The popular and influential cookbook *Le Cuisinier Roïal et Bourgeois* ('The royal and bourgeois cook', 1691), by François Massialot (1660–1733), gave examples of table settings for dinners. Unlike most of the culinary works that preceded it, and as evident in its title, Massialot's book was aimed not only at the upper class, but also at the rapidly growing middle class of artisans, merchants, and potential revolutionaries.

Louis XIV's reign lasted so long (commencing in 1643, when he was just five years old, under the supervision of a regency council) that it was his great-grandson, the conveniently named Louis XV (1710–74), who succeeded him in 1715. Louis XV was a simpler monarch (many claim simple-minded), without his great-grandfather's taste for ostentation. Grandson Louis XV continued to hold smaller dinner parties, while also reducing his staff and the number of dishes served at meals. However, he endorsed the fashionable creation of costly and complicated dishes, giving rise to the half-serious, half-satirical cookbook *Le Cuisinier Gascon*. Written by Louis Auguste de Bourbon (1700–55), Prince of Dombes, and himself the grandson of Louis XIV and his official mistress, it details a mix of actual dishes with funny names ('Frogs in Green Sauce', 'Green Monkey Sauce', 'Eggs Without Malice'), over-the-top edible illusions (veal cooked to imitate donkey

OPPOSITE | W. H. Pyne, *Ancient Kitchen, Windsor Castle* (1818). | ABOVE | Laid table depicted in Francois Massialot, *The Court and Country Cook* (1702). OVERLEAF | Israel Silvestre, *Banquet of the King and Queens* (1664). To celebrate the move to Versailles, Louis XIV held a six-day festival, featuring a banquet based on the seasons.

*Premiere*                    *Festin du R[...]*
                             *plusieurs Prince[...]*
                             *les mets et prese[...]*
                             *quatre saisons.*

Israel siluestre, deline, et sculpsit parisijs.

Reynes auec
més ferui de tous
les Dieux et les

Journée.

et excud. cum priuilegio Regis.

droppings, chickens to resemble bats), and recipes that today read as parodies (ducks roasted only for their juices, to be squeezed over a chicken). It is impossible to tell how much of this cookbook was in earnest, but it surely both exemplifies and mocks the unfettered fabulousness of mid-eighteenth-century French cuisine.

If even cookbooks aimed at the rich were rotten with signs of impending revolt, one can only imagine the putrefaction creeping through Parisian society. In 1757, former domestic servant Robert-François Damiens (perhaps sick to death of serving the nobility ducks squeezed over chickens), attempted to assassinate Louis XV, actually getting so close as to stab him in the side with a penknife. The monstrous overreaction to this attempt that is evident in the roundly incompetent execution of the man by burning and flaying, then drawing and quartering (described in terrible detail by Michel Foucault in the introduction to *Discipline and Punish*, 1975), made clear that

the debauched lives (and dinners) of the royalty were not a charming Renaissance advance, but rather an anachronistic expansion of medieval inequities, gilded by art and technology. No one had been executed in this fashion since 1610, nor would anyone be again.

While French cuisine was emphasizing social inequality, the elite preference for fewer diners helped give rise to restaurants, and a permanent inclination towards intimate mealtimes. The first restaurants opened in the 1760s, and by 1782 they were popular enough for Antoine Beauvilliers to find great success with his Taverne Anglaise at the newly renovated Palais Royale in the Rue de Richlieu, Paris. What the kings hadn't counted on was how useful smaller gatherings can be for plotting revolutions – that is, if people are allowed to talk to one another. Silent meals had never caught on, so when Louis XVI (1754–93) ascended the throne in 1774, he was in charge of a country on the brink of a revolution that was largely being staged at dinner parties. In 1927 Mao Zedong wrote in his 'Report on an Investigation of the Peasant Movement in Hunan': 'A revolution is not a dinner party, or writing an essay, or painting a picture, or doing embroidery.' But how wrong he would have been in eighteenth-century France. Journalist and pamphleteer Camille Desmoulins (1760–94), a notorious hothead whom friends enjoyed riling, became so incensed at a dinner party in 1784 that he leapt on to the table, sending plates, glasses and cutlery clattering and smashing to the floor, and gave a loud, angry harangue on *liberté, fraternité* and *egalité* and revolutionary Republican values. Just five years later, on 11 July 1789, Desmoulins gave a very similar speech from a cafe table at the Palais Royale, which set off a series of riots organized upon his radical principles, and which culminated three days later in the storming of the Bastille and the start of the French Revolution.

By this time, dinner party fashions had actually swung back to progressively larger galas that Louis XVI hoped would give his shaky regime the appearance of seriousness, but so had the size of the revolution. Just as Louis XIV had foreseen and forestalled, large groups of people were rallying to plot the death of the king. Among those who attended numerous dinner parties, where manners were unpicked and philosophies scrutinized to uncover royalist sympathies and hidden venality, were Camille Desmoulins; Louis Legendre (1752–97), butcher and orator; Maximilien Robespierre (1758–94), lawyer and incipient maniac; Georges Danton (1759–94), nascent president of the Committee of Public Safety; and Fabre d'Eglantine (1750–94), actor, poet, and Danton's secretary.

The problem, of course, was that the dinner party was a debauched tool of the aristocracy. Even though it had been thoroughly repurposed as a tool of revolution, its very nature was suspicious. A contrived social situation where divergent personalities are thrown together with alcohol and a backdrop of class warfare: what could possibly go wrong? Two of the primary agents of the revolution, Georges Danton and Maximillien Robespierre, nursed an ongoing enmity that was almost entirely the result of bad dinner party experiences, in which one, usually Danton, offended the other. Whether it was Danton behaving boorishly, making negative remarks about Desmoulins, or, on one occasion, asking a young lady to hold on to a dirty book by the Italian inventor of literary pornography, Pietro Aretino (1492–1556), he almost invariably managed to offend the unrelentingly puritan Robespierre. Even the French-language film *Danton* (1983) portrays a major dinner party fight between these two men. In 1794, a dinner party held to attempt a reconciliation failed, and Robespierre sent Danton to the scaffold the following year. Being violently banned from the dinner party circuit in Paris continues to be referred to as 'being Robespierred' to this day (sadly, this isn't true, but it should be).

Robespierre, as much a master of the treacherous dinner party as Louis XIV, was all ears at these revolutionary soirées, rarely pausing even to eat – a practice Danton had noted and bemoaned. This constant surveillance was to Danton's secretary Fabre d'Eglantine's extreme detriment, when his much-professed love of the playwright Molière (1622–73)

OPPOSITE | An anonymous engraving depicting the public execution of Robert-Francois Damiens (c. 1757). | OVERLEAF | Table settings for thirty guests, from Vincenzo Corrado, *Il Cuoco galante* ('The gallant cook', 1773).

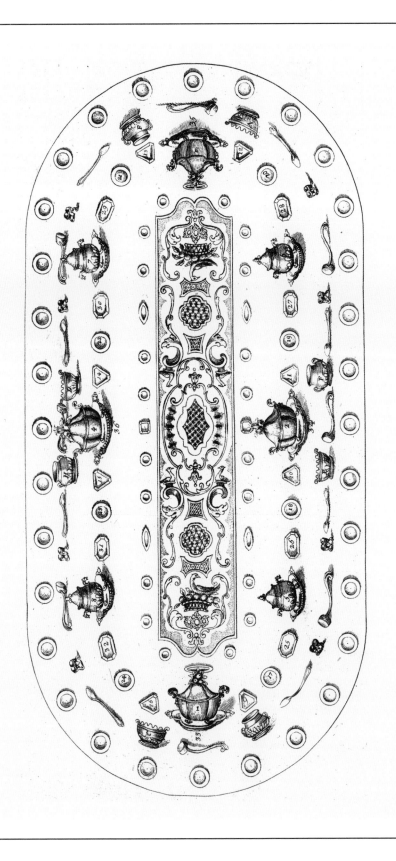

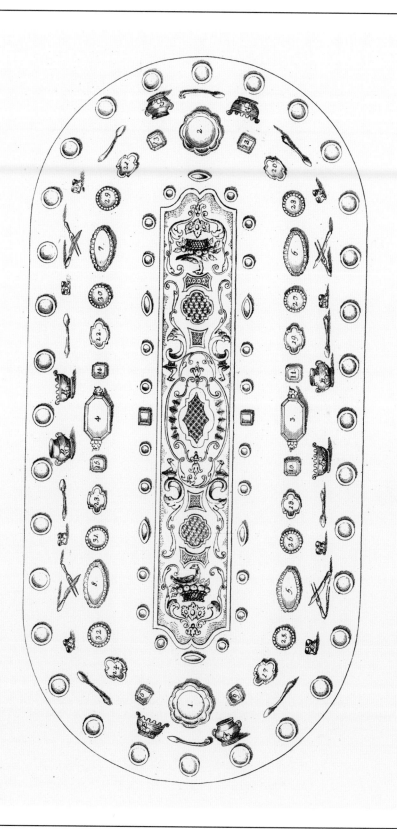

was regarded by Robespierre as proof positive of a dangerous identification with the upper classes and led him, too, to the scaffold. But it could also work the other way: Louis Legendre, who by all counts should have followed, if not preceded, Danton to execution, was spared, due to his constant griping at dinner parties about Danton's luxurious tastes and lifestyle.

The fancy end of the revolutionary spectrum also attended, as you might guess, their share of dinner parties. In the lead-up to the revolution, two of the main players were Honoré Gabriel Riqueti, Comte de Mirabeau (1749–91), a disgraced nobleman who had a second career as a bridge of moderation between the king and the revolution, and Charles Maurice de Talleyrand-Périgord (1754–1838), a bishop and advisor to Louis XVI (and, later, to Napoleon, Louis XVIII and

Louis-Philippe). After the storming of the Bastille in 1789, Louis XVI stepped up his efforts to prevent a complete collapse of his power. On the heels of a large dinner party where the Comte de Mirabeau horrified the wives and servants of the palace with his coarse manners and strange appetites, the royals attempted to recruit Mirabeau to their side at a private dinner party. History shows that they were successful, and that by 1790, Mirabeau, while playing the revolutionary, was working simultaneously for the crown and for Austria. Talleyrand, whose pragmatic and cynical machinations make him one of the most famous political operators in history, could not help but see the writing on the wall. While Mirabeau attempted to line his pockets and take a middle line between burning the country down and maintaining the monarchy, Talleyrand was prepared to be more extreme. Together,

the dinner party to blame for the Reign of Terror and decades of turmoil that followed, as France veered between republic and monarchy?

One figure bravely tried to destroy the dinner party before it caused all of this trouble. Just as the Marquis de Sade's sadisms were, at their root, his attempt to destroy the Catholic Church and everything it stood for, so one man attempted to attack the custom that, like the Church, held the people of France in its sharp claws. In 1783, a lawyer named Alexandre Balthazar Laurent Grimod de la Reynière staged a fake funeral dinner party at which seventeen guests were locked in the house and three hundred spectators were invited to watch from balconies above. It was dinner party as act of violence, intentionally unsettling and unpleasant, with the guests held hostage until morning to eat the variety of dishes (all, allegedly, containing pork). Nearly two hundred years later, the great filmmaker Luis Buñuel dealt with many of the same themes of the violence and degradation at the heart of the dinner party and pursued them with a single-mindedness that would have done Grimod de la Reynière proud. The vacuous bourgeois dinner party that suffers increasingly absurd false starts (*The Discreet Charm of the Bourgeoisie*, 1972), the dinner party as post-fascist hell, at which the participants are trapped in a mansion as their civility is flayed from them, layer by layer (*The Exterminating Angel*, 1962), and the dinner party turned on its head as genteel defecation party (*The Phantom of Liberty*, 1972), suggest that, while the settings might change, the horrors remain.

Of course, had Grimod de la Reynère been more successful, there might have been no Buñuel and no more parties. But the young man, only twenty-five at the time, went too far, too fast, as can be seen in such stunts as his dressing a pig in his

they attended countless dinner parties at which they each made the measure of the other and weighed the rhetoric – and then, it seems, Talleyrand made his move. After a lengthy feast with four other men at Robert's restaurant in the Palais Royale, Talleyrand helpfully supplied coffee and chocolate to smooth Mirabeau's digestion. Directly afterwards, Mirabeau died.

As if to underline that the dinner party was still an institution used by those in power to consolidate and perpetuate their influence over the rest of mankind, Napoleon himself met Joséphine de Beauharnais at a dinner party held in 1795 by her then lover, Paul Barras, leader of the French Directory, to recruit Napoleon in fighting the counter-revolution. Was

OPPOSITE | Jean Huber, *Un diner de philosophes* (1772–3). | ABOVE | An etching and engraving after Jean Baptiste Oudry of an upper-class dinner party in Paris (1756). | OVERLEAF | Advert for the Savoy hotel and restaurant (c. 1900).

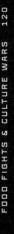

SAVOY
VICTORIA EMBA
"The Hotel de
Magnificent Rive
Bedrooms, single, fro
Special Tariff during Winter
No Gas.    The build
Savoy R
The Fine
Private Rooms
The Opera-Supper is
The Orchestra plays every ev
THE VICT
Specially adapted for Balls, Ban
The ANGLO-AMERICAN BAR & CAFE
Exhibition of Cigars, crops 1888, in o
Cigars.
Chef de Cuisine: M. ESCOFFIE
General Mana

Hildesheimer & Faulkner

DINING ROOM (OAK SALON, HOTEL MÉTROPOLE).

father's clothes to preside over subsequent parties. Said father, exemplifying the notion that humour skips a generation, packed him up and shipped him out to the countryside, where he was forced to sit out the revolution. By the time Grimod returned, he was older and regrettably wiser, and, seeing the promise of restaurants, became their champion. Indeed, he then invented the restaurant review, hopping around Paris to each new establishment, certain that they were the very antithesis of pre-revolution privilege and upper-class stagnation. But were they?

While it's true that restaurants lack some of the more unpleasant characteristics of dinner parties, it is also undeniable that they continue many of the same traditions. When you enter a certain sort of fancy restaurant, or a chain designed to be insipidly pleasant, do you not feel an atavistic shiver of revulsion? Is it not akin to what you feel when you receive a dinner invitation from the Hendersons? Do you not sit in that fancy restaurant and watch people eat, and are you not watched in turn? Everyone is talking – are they talking about you? Probably. The dessert cart rolls by and you can hear Louis XIV, somewhere, exhale. Next time, perhaps there ought to be a picnic revolution.

ABOVE | Dining Room, Oak Salon, Hotel Métropole, London (1901). | OPPOSITE | Frontispiece to Grimod de la Reynière, *Almanach des Gourmands* (1812), showing the 'library' of the gourmand. | OVERLEAF | 'Artistic Arrangement for Dinner Table', Theodore Francis Garrett, *The Encyclopaedia of Practical Cookery* (1892–4).

*Bibliothèque d'un Gourmand*
*du XIX.ᵉ Siècle.*

# CHAPTER SIX

# CROWDSAUCING

The invention of Worcestershire sauce by chemists (John) Lea and (William) Perrins, in the late nineteenth century, has always been cast as a happy accident. The current version of the story goes something like this: mixed according to the instructions of one 'Lord Sandys' who had recently returned from the East, recipe in tow, the sauce tasted terrible and was abandoned in their basement. When Lea and Perrins went to dispose of the barrel some years later, they found that it had miraculously matured into the familiar robust sauce. There was, as you might imagine, much rejoicing.

There are dozens of such food genesis stories involving fortuitous accidents – including mayonnaise, the Mexican national dish *mole poblano*, Reese's Peanut Butter Cups, potato crisps, tofu – and all are unlikely to be true. While I am certain that I will eventually run into such a story that *is* true, in general they were invented to conceal or simplify inconvenient and unwieldy facts.

The English have for centuries conducted a love affair with the glutamate-heavy flavour now known as umami – long before the birth of Worcestershire

sauce in 1837. For much of the eighteenth century, the irreplaceable condiment on the English table was essence of anchovy. This was not lost on condiment expert and sometime poet George Gordon Noel, sixth Baron Byron, who, in his epic poem *Beppo: A Venetian Story* (1817), laments the scarcity of sauces in Italy during Lent:

> *...Because they have no sauces to their stews;*
> *A thing which causes many "poohs" and "pishes,"*
> *And several oaths (which would not suit the Muse),*
> *From travellers accustomed from a boy*
> *To eat their salmon, at the least, with soy;*
>
> *And therefore humbly I would recommend*
> *"The curious in fish-sauce," before they cross*
> *The sea, to bid their cook, or wife, or friend,*
> *Walk or ride to the Strand, and buy in gross*
> *(Or if set out beforehand, these may send*
> *By any means least liable to loss),*
> *Ketchup, Soy, Chili-vinegar, and Harvey,*
> *Or, by the Lord! a Lent will well nigh starve ye...*

'The curious in fish-sauce' to which Lord Byron refers came from an ubiquitous advertisement for Burgess's Essence of Anchovies, a hugely popular condiment in the late eighteenth and early nineteenth centuries, that competed with Reading Sauce (itself mentioned by Lewis

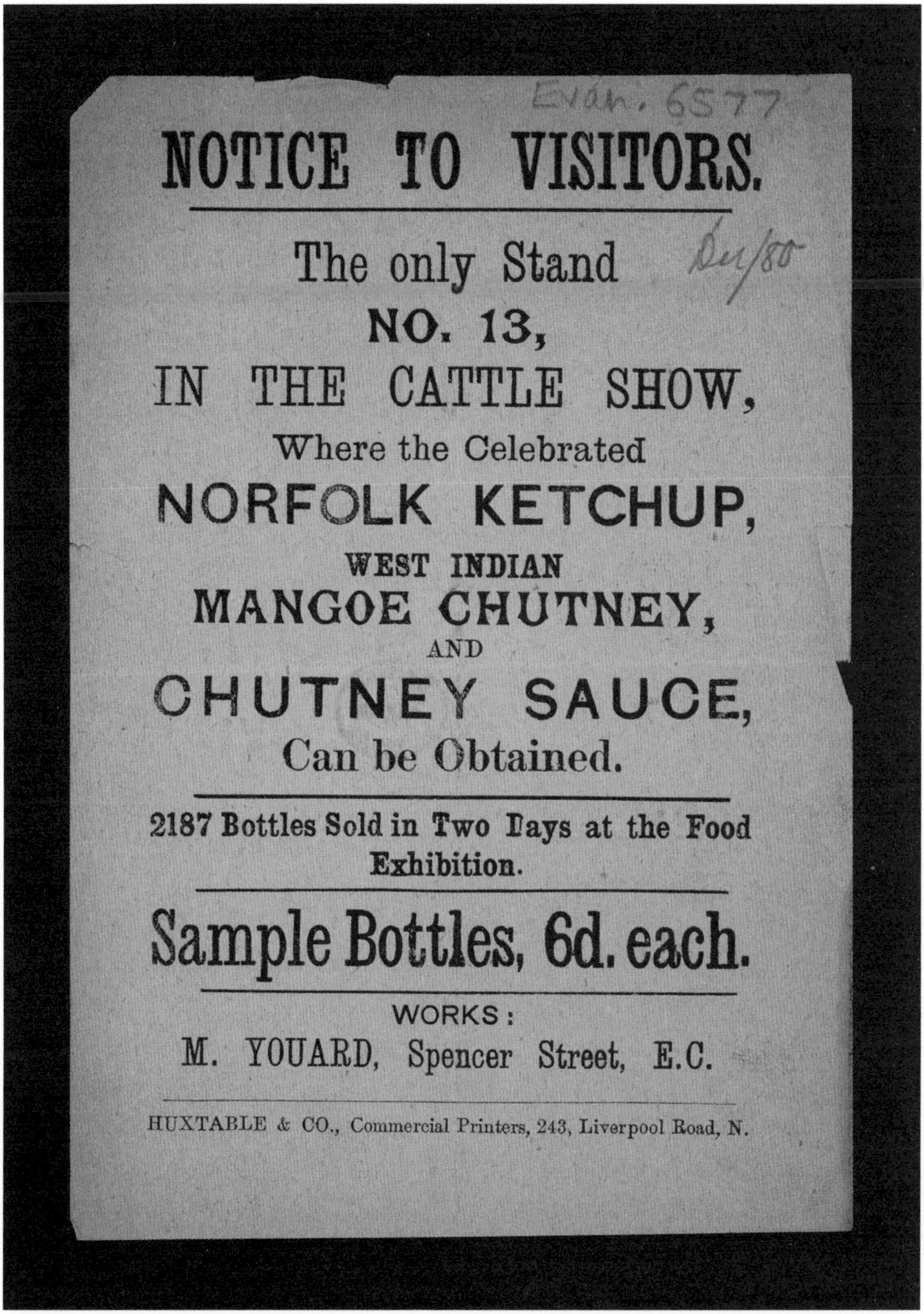

NOTICE TO VISITORS.

The only Stand *Dec/80*
NO. 13,
IN THE CATTLE SHOW,
Where the Celebrated
NORFOLK KETCHUP,
WEST INDIAN
MANGOE CHUTNEY,
AND
CHUTNEY SAUCE,
Can be Obtained.

2187 Bottles Sold in Two Days at the Food
Exhibition.

Sample Bottles, 6d. each.

WORKS :
M. YOUARD, Spencer Street, E.C.

HUXTABLE & CO., Commercial Printers, 243, Liverpool Road, N.

OPENER | *Nursery Rhymes with a dash of sauce* (c. 1920), a small booklet created by the Midland Vineagr Company. | OPPOSITE | Two Victorian ceramic lids for anchovy pastes.

ABOVE | British advert for condiments (1880). Merchants trading with the East India Company brought various 'chutneys' back to Britain, which quickly developed into popular condiments.

Carroll in 1869 in his poem 'Poeta Fit, Non Nascitur', or 'Poets are Made, not Born'; and in 1873 in the adventure story *Around the World in 80 Days*, by Jules Verne) and a bevy of other commercialized, popular-but-now-forgotten fish sauces. Byron also refers to soy (which is, of course, soy sauce, a relative newcomer to England imported from China and Japan), as well as (mushroom) ketchup. Both of these were enjoyed for what is now understood as their concentration of glutamates and powerful umami flavour. Soy sauce was so immediately in demand that home recipes began to pop up all over the place. Making soy sauce at home required forming cakes of cooked, mashed soybeans, allowing the cakes to mould over, drying them, then fermenting them for months: not a quick process, but unless you could pay the high import prices to eat your 'salmon, at the least, with soy', you didn't have a choice. The reprinting and speedy dissemination of this recipe in the first decade of the nineteenth century demonstrates the huge and sudden fashion for soy as the latest glutamic addition.

What links soy and Worcestershire sauces? It has been assumed since at least the mid-nineteenth century that soy sauce is one of the secret ingredients in Worcestershire sauce, which fact seems to have been confirmed in 2009, when an accountant employed by Lea & Perrins rescued an early recipe from a rubbish skip. Worcestershire sauce in England is principally composed of two of the most popular sauce components – soy and anchovy – along with spices and other ingredients, making it not quite as outlandish a concoction as it first seems. In Japan, for example, there is a long history of mixing soy sauce with other liquids to create secondary condiments: *tsuyu* sauce (mixed with fish-based stock, rice wine and seasoning, for noodles),

*ponzu sh yu* sauce (in which it is mixed with the citrus-based Ponzu) and *warishita* sauce (a mixture of salt, sugar, and soy to accompany the beef hot-pot known as *sukiyaki*) all operate on this principle. In England, a recipe from Ann Shackleford's *Modern Art of Cookery* (1767) features a proto-Worcestershire sauce composed of mushroom 'catchup': walnut pickle, garlic, anchovies, horseradish, and cayenne, fermented for a week. So while it's possible that Worcestershire was mixed according to the instructions of a Lord Sandys, an ex-governor of Bengal (whom no one has ever been able to track down), and then accidentally left to age in a basement before miraculously emerging to become one of the world's most recognizable condiments, it certainly wasn't necessary. What was necessary is that Worcestershire survived the bitter sauce wars, trumping Burgess, Reading, and the early ketchups, walnut and mushroom, to give it the appearance of uniqueness.

Worcestershire not only tastes complicated; it *is* complicated. In addition to fish and soy sauces, two fully formed condiments in their own right, the other ingredients combine to form a secret third sauce, similar to that of early Indian curries. This third sauce, concealed in plain sight as complementary spices, might actually be the root of the otherwise-unlikely Lord Sandys genesis narrative. These ingredients – molasses, onion, salt, tamarind, and chilli pepper – would have formed the basis of a fairly representative early Indian curry that could have been

OPPOSITE | Gordon & Dilworth Tomato Catsup trade card (1881). | OVERLEAF LEFT | Extensive instructions for sauces, Hannah Glasse, *The Art of Cookery...* (1747). | OVERLEAF RIGHT | Sauces, Pickles and Bottled Fruits. From Mrs Beeton, *The Book of Household Management* (1892).

# THE
# Art of Cookery,
## MADE
# PLAIN and EASY;

Which far exceeds any Thing of the Kind ever yet published.

### CONTAINING,

I. Of Roasting, Boiling, &c.

II. Of Made-Dishes.

III. Read this Chapter, and you will find how Expensive a *French* Cook's Sauce is.

IV. To make a Number of pretty little Dishes fit for a Supper, or Side-Dish, and little Corner-Dishes for a great Table; and the rest you have in the Chapter for *Lent*.

V. To dress Fish.

VI. Of Soops and Broths.

VII. Of Puddings.

VIII. Of Pies.

IX. For a Fast-Dinner, a Number of good Dishes, which you may make use of for a Table at any other Time.

X. Directions for the Sick.

XI. For Captains of Ships.

XII. Of Hog's Puddings, Sausages, &c.

XIII. To Pot and Make Hams, &c.

XIV. Of Pickling.

XV. Of Making Cakes, &c.

XVI. Of Cheesecakes, Creams, Jellies, Whip Syllabubs, &c.

XVII. Of Made Wines, Brewing, *French* Bread, Muffins, &c.

XVIII. Jarring Cherries, and Preserves, &c.

XIX. To Make Anchovies, Vermicella, Catchup, Vinegar, and to keep Artichokes, French-Beans, &c.

XX. Of Distilling.

XXI. How to Market, and the Seasons of the Year for Butcher's Meat, Poultry, Fish, Herbs, Roots, &c. and Fruit.

XXII. A certain Cure for the Bite of a Mad Dog. By Dr. *Mead*.

XXIII. A Receipt to keep clear from Buggs.

---

### By a LADY.

---

### The SECOND EDITION.

---

### LONDON:

Printed for the AUTHOR, and sold at Mrs. *Wharton's* Toy-Shop, the *Bluecoat-Boy*, near the *Royal-Exchange*; at Mrs. *Ashburn's* China-Shop, the Corner of *Fleet-Ditch*; at Mrs. *Condall's* Toy-Shop, the *King's Head and Parrot*, in *Holborn*; at Mr. *Underwood's* Toy-Shop, near St. *James's-Gate*; and at most Market-Towns in *England*.

---

M.DCC.XLVII.

[*Price* 3 s. 6 d. *stitch'd, and* 5 s. *bound.*]

STORE SAUCES, VARIOUS PICKLES AND BOTTLED FRUITS FOR TARTS AND COMPÔTES.

**SOYER'S SAUCE.**

Sold only in the above bottles, holding half-a-pint.

PRICE 2s. 6d.

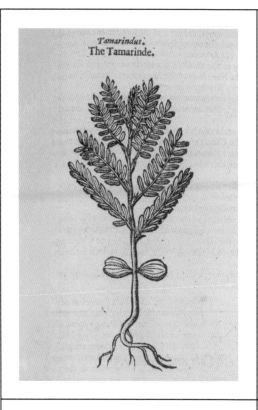

*Tamarindus.*
The Tamarinde.

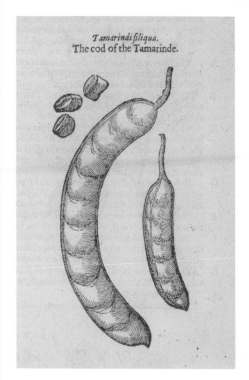

*Tamarindi siliqua.*
The cod of the Tamarinde.

circulating Asia for several centuries. The mythical Lord Sandys and his long-suffering wife, Lady Sandys, might indeed have run into a sauce just like this at many a table during his rumblings around Asia. A diverse and original variety of concoctions for flavouring rice dishes has existed in East Asia for millennia, of which tamarind, an African sour fruit tree long ago brought to India, often forms the heart. In fact, an older (*c.* 1888) version of the Worcestershire Sauce genesis tale has the vaporous Lady Sandys pining for the 'curry powder' that she was used to

in the East (putting aside for a moment the fact that curry powder was an English invention) and a friend helpfully supplying a good recipe that, when added to liquid, became Lea & Perrins Worcestershire Sauce. Perhaps there is a soupçon of truth, however accidental, in these anecdotes after all.

These three Asian sauces – fish sauce (once found throughout Roman Europe, but absent since the 'Dark Ages', and only recently returned as an Asian import), soy sauce (imported from China and, later, Japan), and a tamarind-based curry

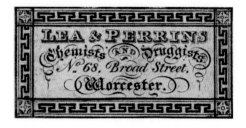

OPPOSITE | Soyer's Sauce (1849). | LEFT Advert for Lea & Perrins Chemists and Druggists, pre-Worcestershire sauce (*c.* 1830). The duo started manufacturing the sauce in the back of their shop on Broad Street in 1837. ABOVE | Tamarind, from John Gerard, *The Herball or Generall historie of plantes* (1633).

sauce – may not have arrived together as Lea & Perrins would have us believe, but they certainly left Asia together. Mercilessly marketed, and well suited to long ocean voyages, they could be found in the hold of every ship bound for every port in the nineteenth-century seafaring world. Lea & Perrins made sure of this, cleverly getting their bottles on board every British ocean liner and offering enticements to stewards to serve Worcestershire Sauce to passengers. Ocean voyages were so prodigiously long, and the food so very bland, that it is no wonder that half the world walked off those gangplanks with Worcestershire-addled taste buds and perhaps a take-home bottle gripped tightly in their hand. Worcestershire Sauce was the first global, virally marketed food. Wherever the British and their ships went, so went this sauce. So what if it made all the food taste the same? The point is that the world's

populace came into contact with this strange sauce and was forever changed, its many palates bending just a little further towards one other. Now we have the Internet to aggregate our opinions, so that people in Kuala Lumpur, Bristol and Lima can routinely feel the same distaste for Justin Bieber, or have the same arguments about the same (white and gold) dress. Yet back in the nineteenth century, anything that recognizable was revolutionary.

As beloved as Worcestershire Sauce was, its watery nature left it inappropriate for use in certain situations. Around the turn of the century, someone had the clever idea to take that third, tamarind sauce, and turn it into a thick, brown sauce: tomato was used as the base, replacing the fish and soy sauces, while still providing some of the umami flavour (tomatoes are one of the richest vegetable sources of free glutamates). *Voilà*, HP Sauce was born. What's funny is that, despite

# The two Sauces of To-Day

## "CHEF" SAUCE

## LAZENBY'S SAUCE

### CHEF SAUCE

is a rich fruity Sauce of recent introduction ; it will be found unequalled with all kinds of hot and cold Joints, Cutlets, Curries, &c

Prepared by
E. Lazenby & Son, Ltd.
18 Trinity Street, London,
S.E.

### LAZENBY'S SAUCE

has for more than 100 years been considered the finest and most delicate Sauce for all kinds of Fish, Game, Steaks, &c.

the lack of a number of the hallmark ingredients of Worcestershire Sauce and the huge difference in use, appearance and viscosity, people have long associated HP and Worcestershire, as if intuiting the family resemblance beneath the strange disguise. What is the relationship between them? Is HP Sauce both parent and child of Worcestershire Sauce, or perhaps its sibling and offspring?

It isn't very surprising that HP Sauce has an accidental genesis story of its own. Edwin Samson Moore, owner of the Midland Vinegar Company, allegedly acquired the recipe in 1903 from Frederick Gibson Garton, who had been selling it as Garton's HP Sauce since around 1895. Despite running the largest producer of vinegar in the world, Moore was making a house call to collect £150, and smelled the sauce cooking in a back room. He was enthralled, and cancelled Garton's debt in return for the recipe. The name

## YORKSHIRE RELISH

### THE MOST DELICIOUS SAUCE IN THE WORLD.

The cold joint, the remains and fragments of yesterday's meat, fish, poultry, or vegetables, may be made into tasty and appetising dishes by the addition of this famous condiment. Its uses in cookery are unlimited, and it is indispensable to the busy housewife.

Sold everywhere in bottles, 6d., 1s., & 2s. each.

DON'T TAKE SUBSTITUTES.

SOLE PROPRIETORS:
GOODALL, BACKHOUSE & CO.,
LEEDS.

OPPOSITE | Lea & Perrins trade cards (c. 1905).
TOP | "Chef" Sauce and Lazenby's Sauce, advertised in *The Graphic*, 8 October 1904. | ABOVE | Yorkshire Relish advert, *The Graphic*, 8 October 1904.

"Hail, Condiment the 4th"

If there is a king of the condiments, it is surely H.P. Sauce. Was ever a Sauce so popular! There it stands with pepper, mustard and salt around it, ready to bestow royal flavour upon the humblest food. If you wish to enjoy the blessings of a hearty appetite and excellent digestion, swear allegiance to Condiment the 4th—

HP SAUCE

Everybody's favourite!

Buy some to-day. Only 9d. the bottle.

MAKE A CAPITAL TEA WITH THE 4TH CONDIMENT

Note the excitement round your tea-table when you put on the H.P. Sauce. Sandwiches become fresh and appetising. Sardines lose their oiliness and gain an appetising flavour. High tea or picnic spread, the 4th Condiment is the best ever for ensuring that nothing is left over.

Pass the HP SAUCE please!

It's only 9d. a large bottle

allegedly came from a rumour Garton had heard that it was popular in the Houses of Parliament. As it travelled around the world, brown sauce began to appear all over the place: in the United States it is the (regrettably) unimproved pre-HP Sauce, A-1 Steak Sauce; in Ireland it is Chef Sauce; in Costa Rica it is the sublime *Salsa Lizano*; and in Australia and elsewhere it has been disguised as species of barbecue sauce.

In the mid-nineteenth century, Japan was restored to Imperial rule under Emperor Meiji. Among the many changes was an increased openness to Western influence and ideas. Inevitably, some of these ideas concerned what to eat, and a wide variety of Western food products and food notions were imported into Japan. As the story goes, one of these was fried pork cutlet or *tonkatsu*, and the eponymous sauce to go with it is a less vinegary version of HP Sauce.

I think the likelihood that *tonkatsu* was introduced to Japan from Europe (by schnitzel-munching Austrians?) during the Meiji period has probably been exaggerated, as the word is written in *kanji* (chinese-originated characters) rather than *katakana*, the script used primarily for foreign words. Given the domestic presence of breaded and fried meats, it seems likely they could have figured out how to bread and fry pork without European intervention. It would be impossible to overstate the popularity of *tonkatsu* sauce. It is used in profusion not just on cutlets, but on vegetable pancakes, soup, stew, noodles and, yes, even rice. People argue over which brand is best and whether it is worthwhile to make your own. The most popular is called Bulldog, meant to evoke English origins and charming foreignness.

So this tamarind-based sauce, hidden for nearly a hundred years as a group of peripheral ingredients in Worcestershire Sauce, went halfway around the world as an Asian sauce imported to England, only to then go all the way back as an English sauce imported to Asia, only to be put on rice all over again. It's a brown sauce there-and-back-again story.

OPPOSITE | Cover of Lea & Perrins cookery book, *Subtle Seasoning* (1932). | ABOVE | H.P. Sauce adverts, *Good Housekeeping*, July 1934. | OVERLEAF | Lea & Perrins advert from *The Graphic*, 8 October 1904

*Lea &*

THE ORIGI

# CHAPTER SEVEN

# CACAO &

# CONFLICT

Chocolate is confounding. The earliest known (*c.* 1200 to 400 B.C.E.) major Mexican civilization, the Olmec, learned the magic of fermenting and crushing the cacao bean to make a thick, fatty beverage. The Maya honed the practice, drinking ground cacao beans hot or cold, with vanilla, chillies, and annatto seeds, for colour and flavour. Cacao has been used as currency, in blood sacrifice, and as a bracing beverage for warriors. It has been fought over, traded, hoarded, bought, sold, marketed, pined after, and eaten to grotesque excess for a thousand years. Can the harmless confection that I put in my children's grubby, supplicating hands really be the potent cacao of legend? How to recognize the favourite treat of bloodthirsty kings, cardinals, and Medicis in this ubiquitous bonbon?

As a double stimulant with food value, the cacao bean is unique in the New World: in addition to much-needed fat, it contains both caffeine and the milder stimulant theobromine. Due to being valuable, easy to transport, durable, and universally desired, cacao beans became the preferred currency of the Mayan Empire. While the rest of the world was going to the trouble of minting gold and silver coins to trade for livestock (how many chickens equals a pig? How to get that half an ox home?), the Maya carried sacks of beans to exchange for goods and services. Can you imagine the potential trouble contained in those beans? It would be like using money in the form of potato crisps sprinkled with cocaine that you could freely collect from tree pods – but tastier. What could possibly go wrong? While the cacao bean grew well on Mayan territory and wasn't hoarded, most citizens were able to drink cacao on a regular basis. Though the egalitarian and peaceful qualities of the Maya have been vastly overstated, they do seem to have been remarkably forward-thinking and benign, compared to other civilizations around that time. It wasn't until overpopulation, mixed with drought, and exacerbated by poor land management, disrupted the empire that, for the first time in recorded history, cacao exhibited what would become a characteristic tendency to generate chaos.

The Mayan Empire, like most empires, had formed by gathering small kingdoms,

cities, and groups under its banner. Their remarkably advanced scientific achievements, organization and flair for the dramatic (see, for example, the ancient city of Chichen Itza on Mexico's Yucatán Peninsula) brought them success, despite building on some of the least hospitable land in the Western world. Though picturesque, the rainforests stretching from Guatemala up the Yucatán Peninsula are notable for their poor soil and erratic rainfall. As the Mayan Empire grew in size and density, so did their reliance on corn and their need for farmland. Mayan construction projects freed up farmland by consuming huge swathes of forest, but caused temperatures to rise and rainfall to dwindle. Did the people start overusing cacao for its energizing stimulants, to try and get ahead with the tree-clearing and temple building? Or did they fight over the cacao itself, as starvation began to provoke border raids on their supplies? Like alcohol, cacao aggregates and intensifies rather than creates, violence and discord, so that its effects are often masked, or emerge obliquely. In this case, cacao found the Mayan people on the verge of starvation, and whipped civil

unrest and stirrings of violence into truly cataclysmic destructiveness. The once-thriving empire collapsed so rapidly that you can still walk through the ruins and survey the half-completed construction projects that were abandoned as the cacao-fuelled revolution took hold. Did they realize that the seeds of their destruction were, well, just that?

After the fall of the empire, life got back to normal fairly quickly. In moderation, and distributed equally across the population, cacao is a refreshing, substantial, and sustaining beverage, but the unsweetened drink of the Maya had little in common with the chocolate milk or hot cocoa consumed today. In a process established in the twentieth century, the cocoa butter and the cocoa powder are separated, with the butter employed only in the manufacture

OPENER | Hernan Cortes landing in Mexico, 1519. Miniature, sixteenth century. | OPPOSITE | Mayan vase depicting a ruler speaking to a kneeling attendant over a bowl of cacao. | ABOVE | Four gods cutting their ears and letting blood flow over cacao pods. Madrid Codex (c. 900–1500).

of solid confectionery, not in drinking chocolate. The Mayan drink used the whole bean, and it is no exaggeration that you can live on the substance. Maya also continued to use cacao beans as currency and, around the turn of the fifteenth century when the Aztec Empire began to form to their west in the great, blasted spaces of Central Mexico, they went to trade. There is no record of whether they intended to disrupt the Aztec, but the Maya were not insensible to the power of cacao: the Mayan deity Ek Chuaj, patron of merchants and cacao, was traditionally depicted as an old man with a sack of goods, but, around this time, he began to be drawn with a scorpion tail and the spine of a death god.

The Aztec proceeded to dole out cacao, now an expensive import, solely to the nobility, while their ever-increasing population barely subsisted on corn. When Hernán Cortés (1485–1587) arrived in 1519, looking uncannily like the white-skinned and bearded god Quetzalcoatl, the well-to-do Aztecs were living life high

on fat and stimulants, while the common people (at least, those who hadn't yet been eaten in sacrificial rites that included the drinking of cacao) were struggling to stay upright in the heat. This was not the perfect recipe to repel an invasion.

In the sixteenth century, the conquistadors brought chocolate back to Spain, where it became popular with the nobility and gradually spread through Europe. By the first half of the seventeenth century, chocolate could be drunk in France, Italy, England, and the Netherlands. It became a favourite of Cardinal Richelieu (1585–1642), who billed himself as the first Frenchman to try the new beverage. Back in the New World, the Jesuits introduced cacao plantations to the progressive 'reductions' settlements

PREVIOUS | Cacao. From from the collection of Sir Thomas Stamford Raffles (c. 1824). | ABOVE | Castle at Tulum, a major pre-Columbian Maya walled city. Frederick Catherwood, *Views of Ancient Monuments in Central America, Chiapas and Yucatan* (1844).

that they were building in Paraguay, which were aimed at converting native populations to Catholicism while allowing them to maintain much of the rest of their culture and language. The reductions produced cacao beans for trade (and to conceal the acrid taste of Jesuit poisons). In fact, after Richelieu alienated Pope Urban VIII in 1642 and then died after a long illness that scholars still have trouble naming (my advice: they should checked his chocolate mug), Cardinal Mazarin, also a chocolate devotee, hired his own personal chocolatier, lest he, too, fall victim to poison. In 1767, the Jesuits were expelled from Paraguay, amid fears that they were becoming too powerful, and their order was dissolved by Pope Clement XIV in 1773. The following year, Pope Clement suddenly died of a mysterious illness. Though histories and fictions have often blamed the Jesuits for poisoning the pope in retribution, we have only his abiding love of chocolate to guide us.

Over in England, in 1649, Oliver Cromwell, the Lord Protector, fresh from doing away with King Charles I (in an apparently non-chocolate-related regicide), responded to early reports of his countrymen's love of chocolate and went to war with Spain. Making an alliance of expediency with the French, Cromwell moved against Spanish possessions in the Caribbean. In 1655, William Penn,

ABOVE | Making chocolate. John Ogilby, *America: being the latest and most accurate description of the New World* (1671). | OVERLEAF | Idols at Copan, Frederick Catherwood, *Views of Ancient Monuments* (1844). PAGES 152–3 | Ek Chuaj in the Codex Borbonicus (*c.* 1507–22). From facsimile of 1899.

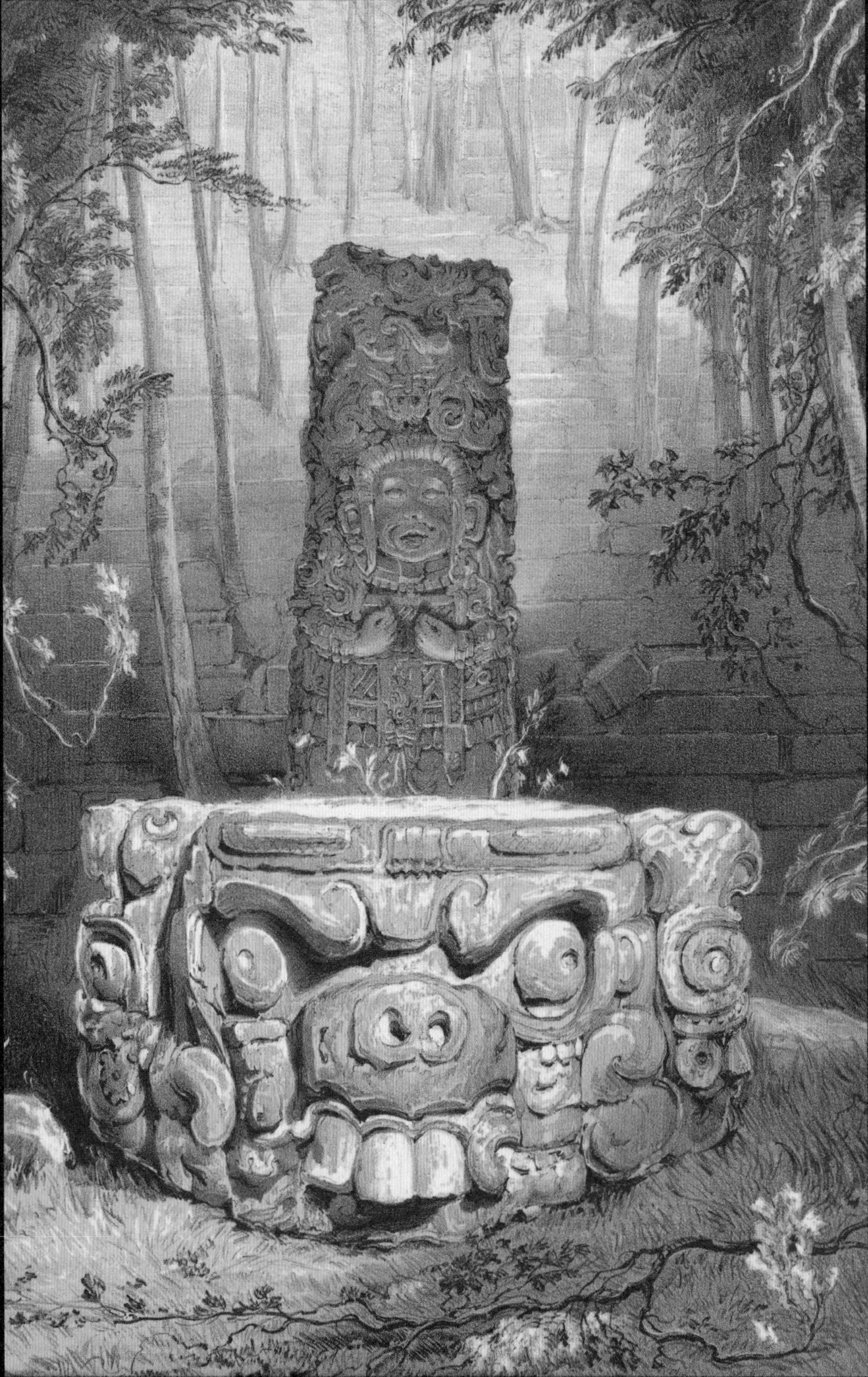

los G aqm̄ nauō
ngadorⁱ

quadecimodia
muerte

endecimodia
culebra

diezmodia
lagartixa

nouenodia
casa

otauodia
muerto

founder of Pennsylvania (incidentally, the future location of the Hershey Chocolate Company), led an amphibious assault on scantily fortified Jamaica, aiming to wrest it and its sixty cacao plantations from Spanish control. Cacao, at the time, was Jamaica's main crop, and it allowed the English to wriggle free of Spain's jealously guarded dominance of the cacao trade and emerge in 1660, at the end of the Anglo–Spanish War, as a major economic force.

The English wasted no time in going chocolate crazy: chocolate houses started popping up like hipster bars in Hackney. The entry of Samuel Pepys's diary for 24 April 1661 records his drinking chocolate for breakfast, having been recommended it as a hangover cure, to settle his stomach. Typically taken hot and sweet, mixed with water, and spices such as pepper, cloves, and anise, the drink quickly rivalled coffee. Unlike the Spanish and French, who treated it as a luxury good only available to the upper classes, the English made it available in shops and cafes to anyone (at least anyone who could afford it, for it cost about twice as much as tea and four times as much as coffee). There were fights and a great deal of gambling in the chocolate and coffee houses, but little in the way of general anarchy. With control of the sugar and cacao supply in the Caribbean, England became one of the world's great trading nations and chocolate drinkers.

Meanwhile, England's gain was Spain's loss. Their continued exposure to massive quantities of chocolate, and insistence on radically unequal chocolate distribution, contributed to the end of the golden age of the Spanish Empire. The chocolate-addled aristocracy repeatedly wrote cheques that the chocolate-deprived ordinary soldier was unable to cash. The Netherlands won their independence and rapidly moved to establish a cacao-trading route via Curaçao in the Caribbean. Once this was

secure, they followed the English pattern of allowing chocolate to be generally available in cafes, rather than hoarding it for the upper classes. The Dutch, after all, had just escaped Spain's clutches, and had seen the dangers of lopsided chocolate distribution at first hand.

Cromwell died in 1658 from an unusually virulent case of malaria, complicated by urinary-tract and kidney complaints. Ironically, chocolate was widely recommended as a cure for urinary and kidney disorders, though the puritanical Cromwell seems unlikely to have been partaking (this was a man who banned Christmas pudding, after all). Did Cromwell relent, only to have his chocolate 'cure' poisoned? If only they had checked when he was exhumed and posthumously executed in 1661. In any case, Cromwell notwithstanding, Dutch and English efforts temporarily suppressed the dangers of chocolate, and little violence can be directly attributed to it

until the end of the eighteenth century. At this point, all hell broke loose.

Concurrent with the Anglo/Franco–Spanish War, in 1648, revolutionary attempts to overthrow the nobility were launched in France. Named Le Fronde (after the slings used to smash rocks through the windows of supporters of Cardinal Mazarin, who was probably trying to enjoy his morning cup of chocolate), the series of civil uprisings failed to topple the system and, in fact, ultimately strengthened the monarchy's resolve for absolutism. Various revolutionary elements were working at cross-purposes, so that they never

OPPOSITE LEFT | Poseidon taking chocolate from Mexico to Europe. Antonio Colmenero de Ledesma, *Chocolate Inda* (1644). | OPPOSITE RIGHT | 'The Coffeehous Mob' fuelled by coffee and chocolate (seventeenth century). | ABOVE | A London coffee house. Anonymous drawing (c. 1690–1700).

developed the critical mass to vanquish the sitting government – just enough to make a lot of noise, and a huge mess. Filled with hubris after narrowly escaping immediate retribution for their misuse of chocolate, the French aristocracy doubled down. A popular late-seventeenth-century cookbook for the monied classes featured a recipe for widgeon stewed in chocolate, as if to say to the people of France 'We are not only going to drink huge quantities of chocolate while you slowly starve, but we have so much left over that we are going to stew cute little ducks in it'. There also arose a craze among the upper classes for anti-venereal chocolates, which you could slip to your wife or mistress to stoke her ardour while also eliminating sexually transmitted diseases. Clearly, breaking point was being reached, and revolution beckoned. Surprisingly, it was North America that went first.

Early in the eighteenth century, the French tried to plant cacao trees in Mississippi and Louisiana, but they wouldn't grow. As a result, American colonies were reliant on the British cacao trade for their fix. By mid-century, Americans had fallen in love with drinking chocolate, and inventor, printer, and military man Benjamin Franklin was already attempting to harness its bellicose powers. During the French and Indian War (1754–63), concurrent with the Seven Years' War between England and France (1755–64), Commander Benjamin Franklin secured six pounds of chocolate for each officer in General Braddock's army.

It didn't take long for the colonies, especially Massachusetts, to begin to bubble over with anti-British sedition. They just needed a final push, which came with the 1765 construction of the Baker Chocolate factory on the banks of the Neponset River in Dorchester, now part of Boston. The chocolate cakes that the factory churned out for the colonists turned out to be more than the already volatile city could handle. The next eleven years saw the Boston Massacre (1770) and ensuing riots, the Boston Tea Party (1773), in which huge quantities of tea were dumped into Boston Harbour by chocolate-loving marauders, and the start of the American Revolution in nearby Lexington (1775). The Continental Congress imposed price regulations to keep the price of chocolate affordable for revolutionaries, and made it illegal to export chocolate from Massachusetts, as it was reserved for the use of the army. Not since 1428, when the Aztec consolidated their power by defeating the Tepanec, had chocolate played so crucial a role in war.

The British, so careful to monitor the effects of chocolate on their island, had failed to police it abroad. Soon, though, they would be more concerned with the grand disorder in France than any situation over the Atlantic. Though both the French and American revolutions were motivated by the ideal of chocolate for all, and inspired by the slowly brewing European Enlightenment, they ran radically different courses. The American Revolution (1765–83) was a relatively isolated event followed by a period of recovery and nation building, while the French Revolution (1789–99) spilled from one cataclysm to the next for twenty-five years. More violent, more progressive, and more ideological than its American counterpart, the French Revolution destroyed the very idea of monarchy and,

PREVIOUS LEFT | Luis Melendez, *Still life with chocolate and pastries* (1770). | PREVIOUS RIGHT | Jean Etienne Liotard, *La Chocolatière* (c. 1745). | OPPOSITE Baker's Chocolate adverts (c. 1924). | OVERLEAF LEFT Trade card for Cadbury's Cocoa (c. 1885). OVERLEAF RIGHT | Fry's Cocoa advert, *The Sphere* (c. 1910).

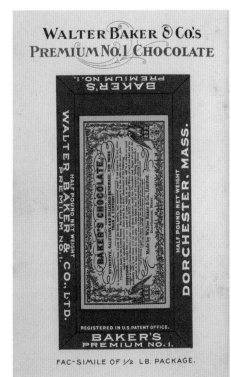

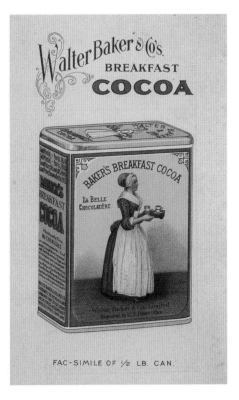

CADBURY'S
COCOA
ABSOLUTELY
PURE.
CADBURY'S COCOA
PRINTED BY W. HAGELBERG BERLIN.

after the Napoleonic period ended in 1815, spread its ideals all over Europe, leading to the vast changes in chocolate production that occurred in the nineteenth century.

The Congress of Vienna was called between 1814 and 1815 to deal with the violence that had cascaded out of the French Revolution and consumed Europe. Borders were drawn and redrawn, and Belgium was carved out and tasked with developing delicious, but violence-mediating chocolates. The new accords, borders, and deeper understanding of the integrity of Europe were represented by the invention in 1832 of the benign and fancy Viennese chocolate cake known as Sachertorte – like the rainbow sent by God after the flood, but more delicious. Following the congress, important steps were taken by the English, Dutch, and Swiss to tackle the chocolate-spawned violence that had for too many centuries controlled the Western world.

The English chocolate makers Cadbury, Huntley & Palmers, Clark's, and Fry's, were all founded within ten years of the Congress of Vienna, and all by Quakers. Propelled by their desire to fend off the slavery that underpinned the cacao trade, and the violence of chocolate consumption, these confectioners invented processes – including the invention of bar chocolate in 1847 – that have successfully blunted the chaos of the cacao bean. Regrettably, Quakers are no longer in charge, and no one has more lately emerged to combat the pervasive and brutal child labour supporting the twenty-first-century cacao trade in Africa.

ABOVE | Advert for van Houten's Cocoa, *The Graphic*, 1904. | OPPOSITE LEFT | Advert for Cadbury's Dairy Milk Chocolate (1928). OPPOSITE RIGHT | Rowntree's New Milk Chocolate, *The Tatler*, 1 February 1928.

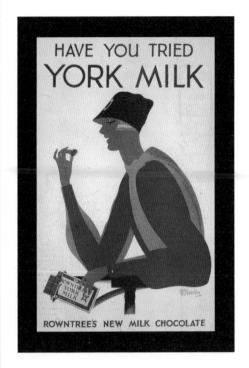

In 1828, Dutch chocolatier Conrad van Houten developed a method to separate cocoa powder from cocoa butter, and his compatriots advanced the process by 'Dutching', or alkalizing, the powder to make it milder. This separation is what makes modern chocolate beverages radically different from their predecessors. Work by the famously neutral Swiss led to 'conching', in which the chocolate is rubbed back and forth between presses until it is smooth and homogenous, causing up to eighty per cent of the volatile aromatic compounds (and moisture) to evaporate. Eventually, these industrial advances produced the sweetly insipid milk chocolate that has become so commercially popular around the world. Processes which add time and heat to the production of chocolate also activate other flavours, and make commercially manufactured chocolate both chemically and gustatorily different to that enjoyed ever before. Though

soldiers were famously sent off with chocolate bars in the two World Wars, those bars were intended to be energizing, uplifting, and symbolic, rather than actually violence-inducing. Appropriately, the amphetamines that were widely distributed to the German army to keep them ferocious and alert during the Second World War, were called *Panzerschokolade*, or 'tank chocolates', by German Panzer-tank crews.

Should you have a taste for proper chocolate, the type with a scorpion tail, then book a trip to Modica in Sicily, where they still make a full-bodied chocolate with the cocoa and cocoa butter as one, painstakingly ground together with crystalline sugar, by hand, at room-temperature. But if you do then find yourself beset by strange urges to throw rocks through the mayor's window and set some tyres on fire, don't say I didn't warn you.

aurum:

# LIFE, LIBERTY, AND THE PURSUIT OF

# CHAPTER EIGHT

# TENDERNESS

# The brovvyllinge of their fiſhe   XIIII.
## ouer the flame.

T he words 'buccaneer' and 'barbecue' share the same source: the Taíno word *barbacòa*, meaning a framework of wooden sticks used to slow-cook, or to dry, meat. A pre-Columbian, indigenous Caribbean tribe, the Taíno specialized in fish cookery, and preserved meat that we would call jerky. It is no accident that the descriptor for the notorious pirates of the Caribbean sprang from the same source word as the term for the outdoor cooking method. At the risk of romanticizing what was probably a grim and unforgiving occupation, buccaneers are the barbecuers of the seven seas: feral, untameable, and existing permanently, and comfortably, just outside of the reach of civilization.

Strictly speaking, barbecue is the cooking of entire animals, or just the cheap, tough parts, for long periods of time at relatively low temperatures, so that the fibrous collagen holding the meat together turns to gelatine – a process that occurs at around 65 degrees Celsius (150 Fahrenheit). To reach this temperature without carbonizing the outside of the meat, the meat cannot be cooked *over* fire (which would be grilling), but merely *near* it, and, usually, in an enclosed space for several hours. In this way, barbecuing is much more like roasting than it is other outdoor cooking practices, such as grilling.

Barbecue's atavistic character gives it a unique place in contemporary Western society. Barbecue is a slow method in a fast

*The broyling of their fish ouer the flame of fier.*  11 3

world; it is cheap in a world obsessed with money; and it is organically social, at a time when reasons to meet fellow humans are becoming increasingly artificial. Though there are people who would sooner barbecue themselves than admit this method can be applied to anything other than their favoured meat, barbecue contains multitudes. It is true that pork has always lent itself especially well to the process. The reasons for this are various, but include the ease and affordability of raising pigs, the deliciousness of the end product, and the high fat content, which allows the collagen time to jellify without the meat drying out. Yet the defining features of barbecue are simply meat, time, fire, and people gathered together to share the delectable results.

In medieval England, until the Enclosure Acts of the seventeenth century began to curtail public uses of common and quasi-common property (such as royal forests), most people owned a few pigs that they would put out to forage for acorns and other arboreal delights, in the ancient practice known as 'pannage'.

The Anglo-Saxons brought the tradition of barbecuing whole hogs to

OPENER | The Luttrell Psalter (1325–1340).
OPPOSITE & ABOVE | Fish cooked over a fire. John White, *Travels through Virginia* (1618). | OVERLEAF LEFT | November, The Breviary of Queen Isabella (*c.* 1497). | OVERLEAF RIGHT | Men beating down acorns for their pigs in November, The Queen Mary Psalter (*c.* 1310).

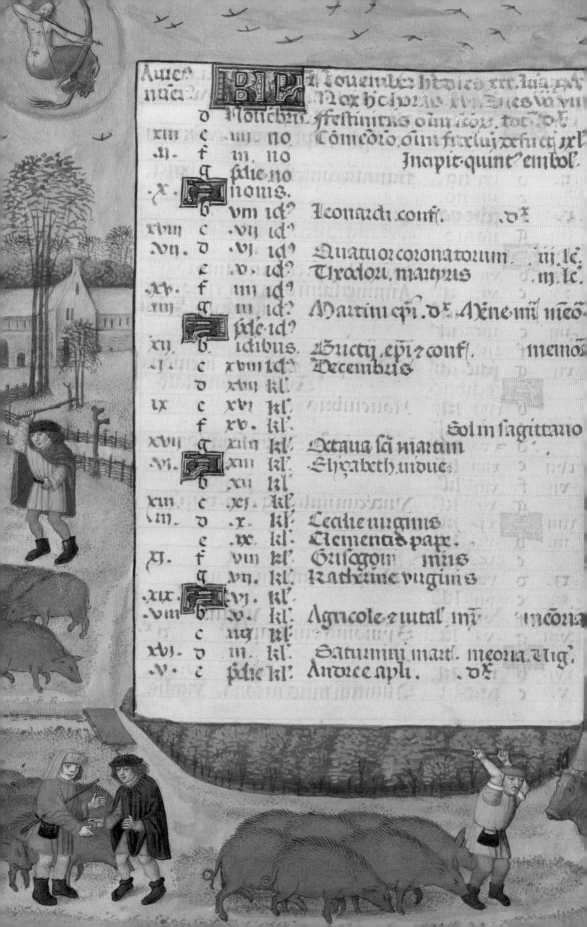

| | | | |
|---|---|---|---|
| | **KL** | | Nouember hꝫ dies xxx. luna xxix |
| | | | Nox hͧ chͤ xviij. Dies vͦ vij |
| | d | Nouembꝛ | festiuitas oͷm scͦ̃ꝝ. tot. DF |
| xiij | e | iiij no | Cõmedͦ oͷm fid̛eliuj defuctͦ | xxl |
| ij | f | iij no | Incipit quintͧ embol. |
| | g | ꝑdie no | |
| x | A | nonis. | |
| | b | viij idͧ | Leonardi conf. DF |
| xviij | c | vij idͧ | |
| vij | d | vj idͧ | Quatuor coronatorum iij le |
| | e | v idͧ | Theodoꝛ martyris iij le |
| xv | f | iiij idͧ | |
| iiij | g | iij idͧ | Martini epī. DF Axͤ̃ne miͥ̃ ntͤoͤ |
| | A | ꝑdie idͧ | |
| xij | b | idibus. | Bricij. epī ꝛ conf. memoͥ̃ |
| j | c | xviij klͧ | Decembꝛis |
| | d | xvij klͧ | |
| ix | e | xvj klͧ | |
| | f | xv. klͧ | Sol in sagittario |
| xvij | g | xiiij klͧ | Octaua sͧ̃ martini |
| vj | A | xiij klͧ | Elyzabeth viduͤ |
| | b | xij klͧ | |
| xiij | c | xj. klͧ | |
| iij | d | x. klͧ | Cecilie virginis |
| | e | ix. klͧ | Clementis pape. |
| xj | f | viij klͧ | Grisogoni mͧrͧs |
| | g | vij. klͧ | Katherine virginis |
| xix | A | vj. klͧ | |
| viij | b | v. klͧ | Agricole ꝛ vital' miͥ̃ ix lcͦna |
| | c | iiij klͧ | |
| xvj | d | iij. klͧ | Saturnini martͧ. ix lcͦna. Uigͧ |
| v | e | ꝑdie klͧ | Andree apͧli. DF |

Scorpi est quintus et tertius est nece cinctus.

| | d | | Kł | Nouemb. Sollempnitas omnium scoz. d.f. |
| xiii | e | iiii | N | Comemozo omnium fidelium defunctozi |
| ii | f | iii | N | |
| | g | ii | N | |
| x | A | ꝏ | | .x. |
| | b | viii | id | Sci leonardi abbis ꝛ conf. iii.lc |
| xviii | c | vii | id | |
| vii | d | vi | id | scorum quatuor coronatorum m̄r. iii.lc. |
| | e | v | id | Sancti theodori m̄ris. .iii.lc. |
| xv | f | iiii | id | |
| iiii | g | iii | id | Sci martini epi ꝛ conf. ix.lc. |
| | A | ii | id | |
| xii | b | | Idus. | Sci bricii epi ꝛ conf. .iii.lc |
| i | c | xviii | kł | Decembris. |
| | d | xvii | kł | Sci magni epi ꝛ conf. ix.lc. |

England in the fifth century, where it became prevalent in rural areas until to the seventeenth century. In Ireland the practice has endured, but is not nearly so widespread as it once was. Likewise, in the northern reaches of the United States, New York, the mid-Atlantic, and New England, barbecuing has largely been replaced by backyard grilling, beyond a few pockets in New England devoted to the clambake (more various than its name suggests, this method involves the slow steaming of seafood, often on layers of seaweed, over hot rocks). In all these places, the climate works against you; the strongest barbecue traditions rely on warm weather, and a relaxed atmosphere that is more difficult to come by up north. As a result, the cookbooks of the Industrial Revolution make the transition to the suckling pig: that familiar picture of a whole piglet with an apple in its mouth, ogling you from a tray of vegetables – a sensible, oven-sized pig for a sensible, oven-centred family.

In the southern United States, however, barbecuing incorporated regional differences and ingredients to become the many-splendoured culture that it remains today. One tradition, introduced by the Taíno and mixed with influences brought by African slaves to the American South, established the pork barbecue and, in parts of Kentucky, mutton barbecue. This practice spread during the Great Migration between 1916 and 1970, as six million African-Americans moved from the rural South to the Northeast, Midwest, and West. The migration was responsible for the distinct barbecue traditions that grew up in Kansas City, Memphis, Chicago, Los Angeles, Harlem, and many other towns and cities across America, as various techniques, sauces and dry rubs from the Deep South commingled with tastes and ingredients in new locations.

The other main influence came from South America, into the Mexican state of Yucatán and then into Texas, to become established as the beef barbecue. One theory is that this was sparked by a meeting between the Mapuche (indigenous inhabitants of south-central Chile and southwestern Argentina, including parts of present-day Patagonia) and the Polynesians (people from any of the over 1,000 islands in the central and southern Pacific Ocean), on Isla Moche, off the Chilean coast. The secret of the earth oven was shared at Polynesian *luau*

parties, perhaps in return for a few baskets of sweet potatoes and a dozen guinea pigs (which had been domesticated and bred for their irresistible deliciousness by the Incas). This method then travelled up the coast, where it inspired the Mayan *pibil* earth oven and the Texan pit barbecue. In mid-nineteenth-century Mexico, middle-class cookbooks such as Gouffé's *El Libro de Cocina* ('The book of recipes', 1893) continued to include extensive instructions for pit barbecuing, evidence of both its popularity and ubiquity. Similar traditions clearly evolved in parallel.

The United States may be home to the most developed traditions, but everyone has barbecued. The Arab Bedouin *zarb*, in which goat and other meats and vegetables are slow-cooked in desert sand ovens, is an ongoing and robust practice. Other regional barbecues, in which smaller cuts of meat are slow-cooked over a low fire, include the Argentinian *asado*, Brazilian *churrasco*, and South African *brai*. These three methods resemble the grilling of meat over direct flames which has become known in contemporary Western societies as barbecuing, but actually retain the essential proportions of temperature and time that turn collagen to gelatine.

Indeed, barbecue was once at the very centre of human existence. Large game would be stalked for weeks before being killed, brought home, and slowly cooked by a huge fire for everyone in the community to partake of the results.

PREVIOUS | Gauchos of Tucuman. Emeric Essex Vidal, *Picturesque Illustrations of Buenos Ayres and Monte Video, etc.* (1820). | OPPOSITE | Cooking on a spit, the Luttrell Psalter (1325–1340). | ABOVE | A Southern Barbecue, from a sketch by Horace Bradley, *Harper's Weekly*, 9 July 1887.

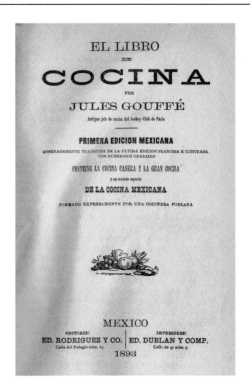

For better or worse, we've moved into a different phase, and the barbecue traditions that remain strong and vibrant are those that exist not beside modern civilization, but outside it. Like coyotes, raccoons, foxes and peregrine falcons, genuine barbecue has found a way to survive, not as the primitive endeavour some people might envisage, nor as the polished, high-tech enterprise some grill manufacturers have tried to foist upon the world, but as a third category: feral and separate. This has left it vulnerable. If it were just a bunch of guys wandering off to set fires and char some meat while drinking beer and banging on drums *Iron John*-style, no one would need to give it a second thought. If it were bringing the technology of the modern kitchen outside to get some air and find a use for that truffle oil, it would concern no one. But a proper barbecue – an open, inclusive, and decidedly *not* a male-dominated affair, as

so often characterizes the first two types – serves as a respite from the world: from both civilization and the chaos that lies beyond it.

Of course, barbecue's popularity has always been the problem. In eighteenth-century North America, it was often co-opted for political purposes. Rich southern plantation owners would throw elaborate barbecues – George Washington famously attended one – with expensive cuts of meat, fancy tableware, and extensive slave labour. These persisted as political gatherings in support of white male hegemony, and it became difficult to get elected without holding a barbecue. In the American South, politicians still view it as important to be seen eating pork and drinking beer with the people. Luckily, making barbecues expensive and easy to attend actually ruins the effect (and, usually, the food). Barbecues are built from time and care, effort and community:

156 wonderful ways to star at your grill and bar!

Seagram's
for wonderful week-end hospitality

SEAGRAM'S WEEK END BAR AND BARBECUE BOOK

making them fancy political events is not so much missing the point as repeatedly running over the point with a truck and then setting it on fire.

This popularity infiltrated the domestic sphere in the early 1950s, as time-saving inventions promised to remake the home as completely and unalterably as the Second World War had remade the world. George A. Stephen at Weber Metalworks in Chicago repurposed the two halves of a steel buoy to invent a kettle-shaped grill that was portable, convenient, and, like most such devices, remarkably disappointing. To be fair to Mr Stephen, I'm sure he only intended to grill hamburgers, hot dogs, and the odd T-bone; all purposes for which his grill excels. But it was the post-war lifestyle and manicured backyard culture that went along with the Weber grill that kept the real thing from catching on. It was just so much easier, especially in suburbia, to

cook on a kettle grill – or, as technology bulldozed forward, a gas grill – on your own private territory. Just as refrigerators and washing machines were marketed to women, so these grills were marketed to men: a Scotch on the rocks, a newspaper, a Weber grill, and 'Let's go out back and grill a few sausages before the game starts'.

In addition to the attempts to appropriate barbecue by upper- and middle-class white men, governments in many parts of the world have made backyard fire pits either illegal, or strictly regulated. In much of the United States you need a permit to set even a beach

OPPOSITE LEFT | A Georgia Barbecue at the Atlanta Exposition, drawn by W.A. Rogers, *Harper's Weekly*, 9 November, 1895. | OPPOSITE RIGHT | Jules Gouffe, *El Libro de Cocina*, (1893). | ABOVE | *Seagram's Weekend Bar and Barbecue Book* (no date, c. 1960s). Illustrated by Joe Kaufman.

fire, and in Mérida, Yucatán, Mexico, it is illegal to roast chillies within city limits. People tend to react to such measures by moving their illicit barbecues to public parks and forests, much as the medieval pigs were set free to forage in the commons. Yet, in our industrialized world, so much more public space has also been enclosed. Digging and making fires are widely prohibited, and grills have been erected in some public parks to encourage people to grill instead of barbecue. The message is clear: grill some hamburgers, burn some sausages, sure, but keep your large, loud, and unrestricted gatherings out of here.

When do these advances and regulations start to impinge upon our freedom? In large swathes of the United States, citizens are preoccupied with the right to bear arms, which is supposedly guaranteed by the (vague and poorly understood) 225-year-old Second Amendment to the United States Constitution. But what of the First Amendment: that is, 'the right of the people peaceably to assemble' – part of the very cornerstone of democracy? Peaceable assemblies need to eat and drink, and if there is a crowd, it makes sense to barbecue. Infringements upon our abilities to provide food for large, peaceful (possibly, slightly tipsy) groups can be understood as an attack not only on democracy, but on what it means to be human – and hungry.

An instructive episode occurred in 1983. Thomas Metzger, a notorious white supremacist and xenophobe, was attending a cross-burning event in

ABOVE | Man sitting outside barbecue stand made of galvanized metal, Corpus Christi, Texas, February 1939. | OPPOSITE | Mobile barbecues in Hyla Nelson O'Connor, *Today's Woman Barbecue Cook Book*, (1954). OVERLEAF | Removing the barbecued beef from the pits, Los Angeles Sheriff's Barbecue (*c.* 1930–41).

Below is Royal Chef grill with electrically turned spit. This can be used also without aid of electricity outdoors with spit turned by hand: for steak, fowl.

Above is special unit made by Androck. Of light metallic construction, it has room on grill for 3 large steaks.

# mobile barbecues

The most versatile kind of barbecue units, these can be just as efficient as the stationary type and yet be used indoors or outside.

The Royal Chef deluxe unit at left features 2 grills. One can be used for steaks or other meats, while fowl or spareribs are barbecued on spit over other grill. In between grills is warming area for bean casseroles, etc. Also has plenty of work-table space.

136

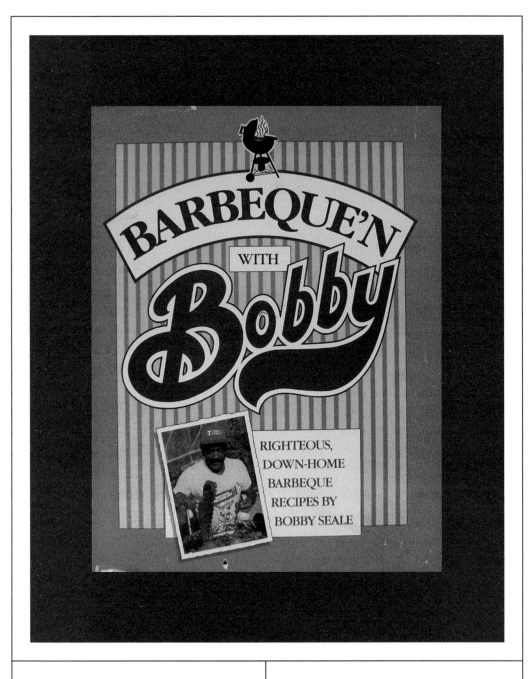

ABOVE | Bobby Seale, *Barbeque'n with Bobby* (1988). Seale's book even contains a Barbeque Bill of Rights: *As the commercialized backwards' bottle-back' recipe methods pursue and invariably evince a design to reduce our backyard-picnics into burnt, half done, bland, badly seasoned, improperly pit-qued entrees, then it is the right of we the barbeque lovers of the world, to alter the cue-be-rab phenomenon and creatively change our recipe process for a more righteous saucy,* *down-home, wood-smoking, delectable, baste-marinating, barbeque'n methodology.*

OVERLEAF LEFT | Domesticated barbecue. A sensible spit for a sensible cook. *Better Homes & Gardens*, June 1960. | OVERLEAF RIGHT | Royal Chef Grill advert, *Look*, June 1954.

Los Angeles. Since Los Angeles County regulations prohibit backyard fires without a permit, Metzger suggested that they obtain such authorization and act under its protection. A freelance writer and photographer posing as a fellow Ku Klux Klan member videotaped them under the pretence of documenting potential police interference or brutality, so there is a record of their incompetence and inhumanity. Now, I am not, like some maniac in an Internet comments section, suggesting that people who misunderstand the difference between grilling and barbecuing are Nazis, but... The members set up a grill, threw what amounted to a pork chop and a can of baked beans on it, and set up their crosses to be burned. A lot of infractions occurred here, and it is worth unpacking a few of them. Metzger was appropriating African-American and Mexican culture – the barbecue, truly a gift to all of humanity – for his grotesque, separatist purposes. Though a racist first, and an anti-Semite second, Metzger had found enough spare time to set up a civilian border patrol just a few years previously to protect America from Mexican immigrants, so he was a reasonably accomplished xenophobe, as well. More importantly for our purposes, though, he was using the government's attempt to control the feral barbecue against humanity.

None of this was lost on Bobby Seale, co-founder of the Black Panther Party, who wrote the part cookbook, part manifesto, *Barbeque'n with Bobby* (1988). Seale argues that the term barbecue is widely misapplied, while also being relegated to holidays and special occasions. He also attacks the restaurants that defame and cheapen the act of barbecue. Seale makes an important and much overlooked point here: what role does commercialization play in the devaluation of barbecue

cookery? Plenty of restaurants serve quality barbecue, but each time another franchise markets factory-cooked meat with 'barbecue sauce', every time another 'barbecue-flavour' snack is rolled out, or McDonald's launches another 'barbecue burger', our agency is reduced a little more. What child browsing a rack of potato snacks would not register barbecue as a flavour, like sour cream and onion, rather than as a vital act of quasi-rebellion against an uncaring, capitalist world, albeit one now so desiccated that it can be sprinkled as a seasoning?

It's not the world's biggest surprise that corporations and governments have been destroying barbecue culture to further nefarious agendas. No, it is as it should be: barbecue has been forced out of range. Attempts to co-opt and commodify only prove the point: humanity and barbecue need one another. It is up to us to exercise some self-control the next time we have a hankering for some ribs: to build a fire instead of ordering in, to dig a pit, invite our friends, acquaintances, and one or two enemies, and stir up a sauce, a marinade, and a rub. As our lives become ever more full of flickering lights, ephemeral sounds, and unmoored notions dancing in our peripheral vision, it becomes more important than ever to take a moment, a breath, a mouthful. Every day we are enshrouded in a digital chaos so complete that it has become a sort of order, and I submit that what it screams for, more than anything else, is a properly made pulled-pork sandwich. All you vegetarians out there, don't think you are off the hook: catch yourself some root vegetables, perhaps a great woolly radish, a tremendous turnip or an outrageous rutabaga. Find yourself a pumpkin the size of a space hopper and barbecue some soup – but take it slowly. S-l-o-w-l-y.

🔺 ABOUT **$24.95**

Cook 30 big steaks at one time on this king-size Royal Chef.

**All Fireboxes Guaranteed**
**5 Years** Royal Chef grills are built to give you pleasure for a long time. With a choice of 12 models, there's a Royal Chef to suit your taste and budget.

Brazier Model RC-66 $34.95*

Brazier Model RC-23 $9.95*

Super Deluxe
Patio RC-338-S $104.95*

**Special Offer -** Write today for Royal Chef's **Outdoor Cook Booklet.** Please enclose 25c in stamps or coin to cover handling charges.

# Cooking's a Picnic Any Time
# on a Royal Chef Grill

Have fun cooking outdoors where everyone can enjoy it---at a party for 30 or with a family of 3. Sturdy, handsome as the picture and twice as much fun, this portable Royal Chef grill features a king-size firebox (16 x 30) with two adjustable grids.

Hickory-smoked steaks with that deliciously different flavor, sizzling hamburgers, southern-style barbecued chicken . . . Royal Chef cooks them all to a queen's taste. See these famous Royal Chef grills and braziers today at your hardware, department or sporting goods store.

**Royal Chef**

*Slightly higher in some areas.*

**CHATTANOOGA ROYAL COMPANY** division of **CHATTANOOGA IMPLEMENT & MANUFACTURING CO.**
Chattanooga, Tennessee
Manufacturers of Royal Chef Grills and Royal Gas Heaters .

# LET THEM EAT QUEQUE

# CHAPTER NINE

In 1838, the French invaded Mexico, ostensibly to collect a number of delinquent debts. The conflict is usually traced back a decade earlier, in 1828, when Mexican troops allegedly damaged a French pastry shop run by a gentleman named Remontel, in the Tacubaya neighbourhood of Mexico City. Alternate versions describe two Frenchmen who may have worked at the shop being murdered by Mexican troops under General Antonio López de Santa Anna (1794–1876), or the troops having simply stolen all the pastries. The story goes that, in 1832, after unsuccessfully petitioning the Mexican government for redress, Remontel complained to the French government and demanded as compensation the outlandish sum of 60,000 pesos (which some have calculated was about sixty times more than his shop was worth). Taking their time, the French eventually decided to add the demand to Mexico's debt, swelling the total amount to 600,000 francs. All of the stories as to why this episode was called the Pastry War fall apart under even the most cursory scrutiny: murder, vandalism, theft, debt – none appear to be true and certainly

none are verifiable. Remontel's petition for redress, as far as history records, was never mentioned in the diplomatic efforts between France and Mexico. Yet one fact is certain; the Mexican people insisted on calling it the Pastry War and have never called it anything else.

Though Mexico had successfully achieved independence from Spain in 1821, its political situation remained in flux for some fifty years, as it was pulled back and forth between republic and monarchy. This situation was not aided by the revolution in Texas that resulted in Mexico's loss of the territory, after General Antonio López de Santa Anna won the Battle of the Alamo (23 February to 6 March 1836) but botched the endgame, and granted Texas independence. It was in the murk of these competing social and political forces that the so-called Pastry War erupted in 1838.

In March 1838, the French anchored a squadron off the coast of Veracruz, and sent an ultimatum from their flagship, the *Hermione*, to pay up or else suffer the consequences. The Mexican government sent back three dozen of their finest *queque* and *bizcochos* (cakes, pastries and cookies)

with their answer: in essence, 'we don't have that kind of cash, and if we did, we wouldn't give it to you anyway.' The French blockaded Veracruz for six months, preventing imports of important trade goods and popular pastry ingredients such as cinnamon, anise, and pineapple. As the diplomatic situation disintegrated, a host of European nations sent ships to look after their interests (that is, to enjoy watching a colony get its comeuppance). Rear Admiral Charles Baudin (1784–1854), a fervent devotee of *Charlotte à la Parisienne*, was appointed by the French to take charge of the fleet. He brought along his own pastry chef, probably a disciple of Marie-Antoine Carême (1784–1833), the world-famous French chef, inventor of the *Charlotte à la Parisienne*, and author of *Le Pâtissier Royal Parisien* (published in English, in 1834, as *The Royal Parisian Pastrycook and Confectioner*), which features his *pièces montées*: cake designs so elaborate that they often resemble military fortifications.

Though printing in Mexico dates back to the sixteenth century, the first two Mexican cookbooks were printed in 1831, a decade after it won independence from Spain. Both *Novisimo Arte de Cocina* ('New Art of the Kitchen') and *El Cocinero Mexicano* ('The Mexican Cook') were attempts to create a national food identity: the first tentatively, the second with substantial force of rhetoric and recipe selection. *El Cocinero Mexicano* contains six sections of sweets with a total of around eight hundred recipes, very intentionally proposing a distinctive cuisine for a newly independent Mexico. For hundreds of

OPENER | Jules Gouffe, *The Royal Book of Pastry and Confectionary* (1874). | OPPOSITE TOP | General Santa Anna. Lúcas Alamán, *Historia de Méjico* (1849–52). OPPOSITE BOTTOM | The attack on the home of General Santa Anna, 1838. Watercolour *c.* 1870. ABOVE | View of Vera Cruz, from *México y sus alrededores* (1869).

Cascade égyptienne.

Tour de Rhodes.

Fontaine antique.

Grand Pavillon chinois.

Ruine d'un château fort.

Fontaine Turque.

Ecole à la française.

Pavillon gothique de treilles.

Ruine gothique.

Detailed architectural models
for unlikely pastry confections.
Marie-Antoine Carême,
*Le pâtissier pittoresque* (1842).

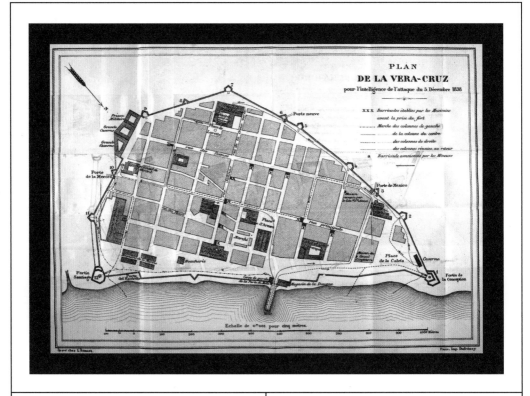

years, Spanish colonists had come to Mexico expecting to satisfy their sweet tooth and this presumption, along with native ingredients such as chocolate, vanilla, strawberries, black cherries, and prickly pears, built a robust tradition of sweet courses. There was a quasi-European pastry tradition, usually dominated by male chefs (in the Spanish fashion) using local ingredients and dictated by local sensibilities. Parallel to this largely male tradition, was one of cakes made in convents, by nuns. This was the Mexico in which Remontel opened his pastry shop, serving, no doubt, the very cutting edge of Marie-Antoine Carême-inspired architectural delights and miniature masterpieces. In this brave new Mexico, many hundreds of varieties of sweet courses made with local and European methods and ingredients had steeped and blended together as they were passed around in manuscript copies for 250 years,

evolving into something wholly syncretic and unique.

On 21 October 1838, fleet commander Charles Baudin sent a message that precipitated a second meeting with the Mexican foreign minister, Luis Cuevas: this time in Veracruz's state capital, Xalapa, on 17 November. The Mexicans, starved of their usual range of pastries, were undoubtedly more eager to come to an agreement, but the French decided to tack on 200,000 additional pesos to cover their costs (for example, having brought a pastry chef across the Atlantic). Cuevas refused, perhaps thinking, 'We've survived on chocolate and vanilla *bizcochos* before, how bad could it be?', but likely discounting, as he was from Mexico City, just how important the busy port of Veracruz was to the local economy: with the port blockaded, there would be no *leche de piña* (pineapple milk) or *cubiletes de canela* (cinnamon pastry). The French moved three frigates, a corvette, and two bomb vessels into position, and waited for word from France and the somewhat surprisingly named Comte Louis-Mathieu Molé (1781–1855), Prime Minister of France.

Earlier that year, an Austrian ex-artillery officer and entrepreneur named August Zang (1807–88) founded a bakery, the Boulangerie Viennoise, on Rue de Richelieu, in Paris. He served assorted Viennese specialities, but his signature was his own invention: a buttery, flaky, crescent-shaped roll he named the *croissant*, based on the similarly shaped vanilla-almond cookies called *kipferl*. The French descended upon the boulangerie and made off with the croissants, the recipe, and the very idea, leaving a violently upended tray of *kipferln* in their wake. Did Count Molé immediately send a box of these new, wildly popular, croissants to Baudin along with his instructions? Probably not, but it would have been a nice gesture.

On 27 November 1838, Mexican envoys boarded Baudin's ship with a last-minute conciliatory offer, but were rebuffed after only a few hours of discussion. The shelling began immediately, while the dignitaries were still making their way back to the harbour. The harbour's castle, San Juan de Ullúa, was manned by 1,186 soldiers with 153 guns, but they proved no match for the brand new shells developed by French artillery officer Henri-Joseph Paixhans (1783–1854), a great lover of *soufflés au parfait-amour* ('perfect love', an alcoholic syrup flavoured with flower petals, vanilla, and orange peel). Their flat trajectory and tremendous punch meant that the battle was short and decisive. After the first afternoon of shelling, in which the French lost 4 men and the Mexican defenders 224, Baudin informed the castle commander that his next trick would be to reduce the castle to a pile of smoking rubble. The garrison commander and the

general in Veracruz conferred, after which they decided that perhaps they could dig around in their sofas and find that money after all. It was agreed to lift the blockade for eight months, and Baudin's men were allowed ashore to refresh provisions and sample a delicious *budin de leche* (milk pudding). Except that's not what happened: when word got back to Mexico City of the capitulation, the general and garrison commander were arrested, and Santa Anna, who had come out of retirement to combat the French threat, was ordered to attack. Perhaps crucially, Santa Anna was not a huge fan of pastry, but was so very fond of roast chicken that he was captured by North Americans on 18 April 1847 at the Battle of Cerro Gordo, when he chose to linger over his chicken rather than retreat.

OPPOSITE | Plan of Vera Cruz, in preparation for the attack on 5 December 1838. | ABOVE | Simón Blanquel, *Novisimo Arte de Cocina* (1831).

By the time of the Pastry War, French cuisine (with a little help from Napoleon) had already run roughshod over most of Europe's culinary heritage. The French were used to countries rolling over and accepting the superiority of their food, so when Mexico spurned their croquembouche, pains-au-chocolat and madeleines aux pistaches, their answer was to break out their second favourite invention: artillery.

Baudin and Santa Anna scheduled the recommencement of hostilities for 8 a.m. on 5 December 1838, and each retired: Baudin to his madeleines, Santa Anna to his chicken. But Baudin decided to launch his assault a few hours early. Santa Anna was caught unawares (that is, asleep) as Baudin's men swept through town, taking square after square before settling in to repeatedly fire small arms at the reinforced barracks doors. When this didn't work, Baudin waved the white flag to once again signal a cessation of hostilities. Santa Anna, who narrowly

escaped from his home as the French troops swarmed by and was still smarting from the humiliation, chased the French back to the docks, where he and his men were hit by artillery fire from the anchored frigates. Santa Anna lost nine men, his left leg below the knee, and a finger on his right hand (cruelly, his sauce-tasting finger). Baudin, angry that his white flag had been ignored, causing him to lose eight men, shelled the city for two hours solid.

Santa Anna went on to have his prosthetic leg stolen from him by the 4th Illinois infantry during the roast chicken episode of 1847. Though the Mexican government repeatedly tried to get the leg back from the United States government, even going so far as to offer to officially declare doughnuts to be 'at least as good as *buñuelos*', you can still visit the leg in the Illinois State Military Museum. The signature dessert in Illinois is the brownie, which was invented for the Chicago World's Fair in 1893... but I digress.

The British, who, you remember, were nearby, protecting their interests, stepped in to calm things down, and despite the fact that the Admiral Sir Charles Paget's (1778–1839) favourite treat was blancmange, managed to negotiate a ceasefire and, ultimately, a treaty, on 9 March 1839. The specific details of the treaty are unavailable, but Mexico's culinary heritage remained strangely linked to France for the rest of the century. Many popular Mexican cookbooks were published in Paris, including the popular and influential *Nuevo Cocinero Mexicano en Forma de Diccionario* ('New Mexican Cook in the Form of a Dictionary'), which was first published there in 1845, and still published in Paris until 1903. Marie-Antoine Carême and his sometime writing partner, the restaurateur Antoine Beauvilliers (1754–1817), are invoked on the title page, and within the book much of traditional Mexican cuisine is derided as the food of poor people. This prejudice extended northward, so that Mexican immigrant Encarnación Pinedo

(1849–1902), writing the first Spanish language cookbook in the United States, *El Cocinero Español* ('The Spanish Cook', San Francisco, 1898), extols French chefs, calling them 'the best cooks in the world'. The effects of French culinary colonialism lingered into the twentieth century – you are still more likely to find a French than a Spanish restaurant in Mexico City – but have dissipated with time. Between the 1930s and 1960s, Josefina Velázquez de León (1905–68) published a series of cookbooks that put regional Mexican cuisine at the forefront and changed the narrative forever. The Pastry Battle may have been lost, but the war was won, more or less, in the end.

OPPOSITE | Sponge cake glazed a l'Italienne, Croquembouche of Almonds and Pistachios. Jules Gouffe, *The Royal Book of Pastry and Confectionary* (1874). ABOVE | Horace Vernet, *Épisode de l'expédition du Mexique en 1838* (1841). The explosion of the tower of the Fort of Saint Jean d'ulloa on 27 November, 1838.

# COCINA MEXICANA DE ABOLENGO

### POR *Josefina Velázquer de León*

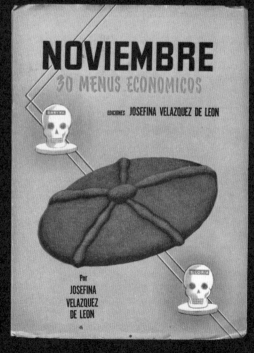

**OPPOSITE & ABOVE** | Cookery books published by Josefina Velasquez de León. | **OVERLEAF** Architectural confections from Jules Gouffe, *The Royal Book of Pastry and Confectionary* (1874).

Pl. VI.

ITALIAN VILLA MADE OF NOUGAT

*Pl. VII.*

RUSTIC SUMMER, HOUSE

# THE

# CHAPTER TEN

THICKENING

There was a time when viscosity, or 'thickness', was simply a quality that food had in various measure. Your meal might be appropriately thick (such as gruel, aspic, or blancmange), or inappropriately thick (as in broth, or beer soup), but no particular value judgement was attached to thickness itself, any more than it is to 'beigeness' or 'roundness'. Food was judged on its own merits, rather than whether it represented an arbitrary level of viscosity associated with luxury or satiety. Many changes in food over the centuries are the result of shifting ingredients, trade routes, imperialism, capitalism, fashions and technologies, but only a few are caused by all of these at once. This is the story of how modern liquid foodstuffs became so very thick.

In the Middle Ages, most sauces and condiments were relatively thin. The most common thickeners, breadcrumbs and (weirdly and expensively) ground almonds, simply weren't practical for the purpose, because both tend to make more of a slurry than a viscous sauce. Many of the most desired and popular sauces – such as the cinnamon and vinegar sauce cameline, the parsley sauce known as green sauce, and sauce agraz, made from verjuice (wine made from unripe grapes) – were quite runny. The gravy (which consisted only of meat juices) in meat pies was so highly prized that gravy thieves would contrive to steal and reuse it by drilling holes in the bottoms of the pies. These brigands were so common that in 'The Cook's Prologue and Tale' from *The Canterbury Tales* (c. 1390), Geoffrey Chaucer (1343–1400) portrays his scurrilous cook as just such a fraud, letting the 'blood' out of pies before reselling them:

> *For many a pastee hastow laten blood*
> *and many a Jakke of Dovere hastow sold*
> *That hath been twice hoot and twice cold*

'Dover[e]' was slang for 'do-over', so that a 'Jack of Dover' might be an expensive bottle of wine refilled with plonk, or a pie that had been cooked more than once. The phrase was so common that, a century later, proto-communist Sir Thomas More (1478–1535) had shifted the blame across the English Channel, in referring to 'A Jak of Parys, an evil pye twyse baken'. It remains unclear what part

*The Cokis tale*

OPENER | Bisto advert, 1929 | LEFT | The Cook's Tale, Geoffrey Chaucer, *The Canterbury Tales* (1492). OPPOSITE | Canterbury Pilgrims, from the prologue to the *Canterbury Tales* (1492). | OVERLEAF | Corn and potatoes, John Gerard, *The Herball or Generall historie of plantes* (1633).

Ret chere made our oft to bs euerychon
And to fouper fette he bs anon
He ferued bs wyth bytaple at the befte
Stronge was the wyne ʒ wel drynke bs lyfte

A femely man our ofte was wyth alle
Forto be a marchal in a lordes halle
A large man he was wyth eyen ftepe
A feyrer burgeys is ther non in chepe
Bolde of hys speche and wel was y taught
And of manhoode lacked he right nought
Eke therto was he right a mery man
And aftir fouper to pleyen he begon
And fpak of myrthe amonge other thynges
Whan that we hadde made our rekenynges
He fayd thus now lordynges treuly
Ye be to me right welcome hertly
For by my trowthe yf I fhal not lye
I fawe not thys yeer fo mery a companye

# The forme of the eares of Turky Wheat.

### 3 *Frumenti Indici spica.*
Turkie wheat in the huske, as also naked or bare,

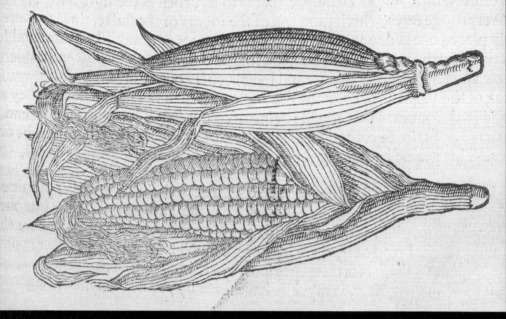

# Chap. 349. Of Potato's.

*Sisarum Peruvianum, siue Batata Hispanorum.*
Potatus, or Potato's.

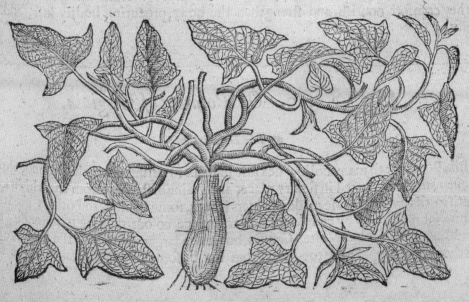

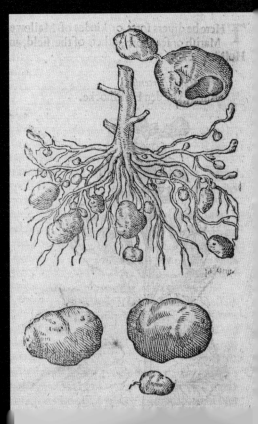

this played in the Anglo–French War of 1512–14.

In fact, it wasn't until Europe's colonial era that the vogue for adding thickeners to food took hold. As European powers successfully subjugated native populations and made them grow the sugar, spices, and other crops that had been shuffled around the globe, they also discovered a host of new crops, containing starches that could be used as thickeners. Arrowroot from the Caribbean, tapioca from Brazil, *katakuriko* from Japan, potato starch from South America, corn starch from North America, and sago from New Guinea were all 'discovered' and commercialized during the sixteenth to eighteenth centuries. These additives were especially useful in making the aspics, jellies, and flummeries that became so popular in the seventeenth

century. Napoleon, not one to miss an opportunity to poke fun at the English, famously made the acute observation that the only reason the British ate so much arrowroot was to support their overseas colonies.

Indeed, the relationship between overseas slave plantations growing huge supplies of food for European consumption and the demand emerging for that food is very muddled. Flann O'Brien (1911–54) wrote a very amusing fragment of a novel called *Slattery's Sago Saga*, in which he describes an attempt to grow sago in Ireland to replace the potato, itself a South American import intended to replace the turf that the Irish had blithely been eating for centuries. The perpetrator of this plan is a Scottish woman who intends to cleanse Ireland of indolence and to stop Irish emigrants from spreading their popery all over the world. Ireland is positioned at the terminus of the Gulf Stream, where O'Brien contends that palm trees will thrive, providing the new starchy backbone of the Irish diet and making Ireland look more like a proper English colony – funny, yes, but also right on the nose. Those imported starches that made the biscuits and jellies for serving at dinner parties were, of course, also being used to feed the increasingly numerous engines of the Industrial Revolution. Whether you consider the potato in northern Europe, or corn polenta in Italy, colonial starches were keeping the peasantry alive and working, if sometimes barely.

This conflation of thickener and capitalism did not become less complicated as time went on. In the eighteenth century, the English were beginning to adopt French cuisine. Gravy had always been presumed to consist of the juices produced by cooking a large piece of meat. By the middle of the eighteenth century, this had changed forever, as a potent and expensive French sauce began to erode the English-speaking world's very concept of gravy. Ironically, the perpetrator of this change was the author of *The Art of Cookery Made Plain and Easy* (1747), the famously French-baiting English cook, Hannah Glasse (1708–70):

> *So much is the blind folly of this age,*
> *that they would rather be impos'd on by*
> *a French booby than give encouragement*
> *to a good English cook.*

In a rambling introduction to her enormously successful cookbook, Glasse, the most central figure in British cuisine until Mrs Beeton made repeated attacks on French cuisine as overwrought, expensive, and pretentious. In a detailed attempt to replace what she had construed as French gravy – but was actually sauce espagnole – she suggests substituting bacon for 'ham essence', using less veal, some beef, a pigeon rather than a partridge, and an array of vegetables including onions, carrots, truffles, and morels to make a more sensible sauce that will 'save the ladies a great deal of trouble'. Rather than dissuading the three or four English cooks who were inclined to do so from making a proper sauce espagnole to enhance their roasts, she instead succeeded in creating a new standard for gravy: thick, rich, and expensive. All gravy-making cooks since then have striven for this Platonic ideal, whether they knew it or not.

Yet it's an impossible ideal, for all the same reasons Hannah Glasse outlined in her misguided attack on 'French gravy'. Many ordinary cooks were unable to make either a proper sauce espagnole or Glasse's slightly-cheaper-but-still-enormously-expensive and time-consuming facsimile, but they could yearn for such a sauce, and yearn they did. Just a few decades later, you begin to see the construction 'thick and rich' proliferate in English and American food culture. The first mention of a flour roux appears in 1793, in the English translation of a French cookbook: Menon's *French Family Cook*. Thickness

---

OPPOSITE LEFT | Gum plants – Gum Arabic, Gum Traganath, Gum Olibanum, Gum Mastic. From William Rhind, *A History of the Vegetable Kingdom* (1857). OPPOSITE RIGHT | Plants used as Food – Arrowroot, Manioc or Cassava, Yam, Sweet Potato.

OVERLEAF LEFT | Sago tree. François Pierre Chaumeton, *Flore Médical* (1814–20). | OVERLEAF RIGHT | Jellies, Creams and Sweet Dishes. Mrs Beeton, *The Book of Household Management* (1892).

Turpin P.t                    Lambert f.t Sculp.

SAGOU.

a. b. l.

Jelly of 2 Colours.

Macedoine of Fruits with Jelly.

Lemon Cream.

Victoria Sandwiches.

Meringues.

Grape Jelly.

Trifle.

Chocolate Cream.

Iced Oranges.

Stewed Pears.

Tipsy Cake.

Rout Cakes.

Crystalized Fruits.

Nougat Almond Cake.

Apples à la Parisienne

Blanc-Mange à la Vanille.

becomes a byword for satisfying wealth and comfort: rich brown flavours stand for sated evenings spent by the fire. The two ideas, thickness and richness, became so synonymous that you might reasonably expect to have seen Industrial-Age magnates with cigars and top-hats as brown blobs that oozed through the streets. Throughout the nineteenth century, gravy and other sauces start to be described in cookbooks in terms of their viscosity – thick as cream, thick with eggs, thick with flour, thick as batter – rather than their essential characteristics. A popular 1899 cookbook suggested adding arrowroot, should your tomato sauce be too thin, and a somewhat laborious joke from an 1841 edition of the weekly British magazine *Punch* describes gravy so thick that were you skating on it, you would not fall through. As viscosity spread from gravy to all kinds of sauces and condiments, new methods of thickening were called for. The lower and middle classes had been sold on thickness and were swaddling that gravy blanket around themselves like it was the affluence and comfort that they were increasingly unlikely to realize.

As industrialization proceeded apace, both methods of thickening and simulations of idealized gravy became increasingly complex. At first, the influx of new starches and imported roux techniques were sufficient to keep viscosity addicts sated. Then came Bisto, the popular British brand of gravy granules that was launched in 1908, which employed wheat and potato starch as thickening agents, along with yeast powder to add meat-simulating glutamic flavour. For salad dressings, bottled condiments and, more recently, modish low-carb gravies and sauces, a thickener that was also an emulsifier was needed, and one which did not break down to sugar, as starch does.

Since the Middle Ages, a number of tree saps were used to thicken and stabilize certain recipes. Tragacanth gum was recommended in a famous sixteenth-century recipe favoured by the French apothecary and seer Michel de Nostredame (1503–66), better known as Nostradamus, for making plates and cups from sugar. Gum arabic is still used in certain desserts, and guar and locust bean gums are among others still commonly used in food production. However, most of these gums were either too difficult to source to be used in bulk for common recipes, or not quite suited for their intended applications.

Nowhere was the need for a thickener

more keenly felt than in the United States. In the mid-twentieth century, the United States was falling behind, not only in the Space Race, as the Soviet Russian cosmonaut Yuri Gagarin was launched into the stratosphere in 1961, but also in the thickness race. Russians were happy to add sour cream to everything, but the United States was finding it difficult to bridge the viscosity gap that was threatening to swallow the hopes and dreams of post-war America. Once again, capitalism came to the rescue: in jumped the United States Department of Agriculture.

Just as bouillon cubes and Marmite were invented in the early-twentieth century to put food tasting approximately of meat into the hands of those who couldn't afford it, so thickeners were researched to ply the populace with soul-soothing sauces, so that their gravy would match their thickening post-war midriffs. In the early 1960s, following both the Cuban Missile Crisis and Gagarin's rocket launch, the United States

Department of Agriculture discovered that a polysaccharide excreted by a plant disease-causing bacterium called *Xanthomonas campestris* made a terrific thickener and emulsifier when dried. Thus was born one of the great products of the twentieth century and the world's most versatile thickener: xanthan gum. Did it win the Cold War? Opinions are split, but on balance, I'd say 'probably.'

It should surprise no one by now that these gums and thickeners are further entwined with the march of capitalism.

OPPOSITE | Symington's Pea Flour advert. *The Graphic*, 1904. | ABOVE | Advert for Brown & Polson's Corn Flour in Marguerite Fedden's *Empire Cookery Book* (1927) – a book compiled to encourage the consumption of produce from around the British Empire. | OVERLEAF LEFT | New Dream Whip won't wilt (thanks to modified cornstarch and cellulose gum). *Better Homes & Gardens*, March 1960. OVERLEAF RIGHT | Xanthan gum in action. *Better Homes & Gardens*, January 1960

# Enjoy all you want

New Dream Whip is low in cost, low in calories—only 17 per serving. And so easy to mix—just add milk, vanilla, and whip. Comes in a box (big new double size or regular), stays fresh on your shelf, needs no refrigeration. Won't wilt, won't separate, keeps for days.

Just add milk, vanilla and whip

# NEW DREAM WHIP

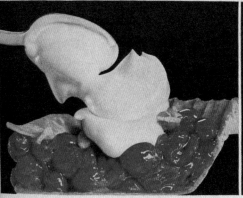

Light and lovely Dream Whip makes pies and puddings twice as fancy. And you can use it for days—stays fresh in the refrigerator.

Cherry Dream Cake is the easiest dessert ever! Simply layers of sponge cake...chopped cherries...and luscious new Dream Whip.

Snowy Pears—with Jell-O. Pear halves...soft Jell-O gelatin spooned on...and a mountain of Dream Whip. Added calories? Hardly any.

Dream Whip on anything costs so little. Like on gingerbread cake. You can heap it high with never a thought for the budget.

Tested by General Foods Kitchens. Jell-O and Dream Whip, trade-marks of General Foods Corp.

**JELL-O**
**BRAND**
**PUDDING** *and*
**PIE FILLING**

**VANILLA**
FLAVOR
JUST ADD MILK
MAKES ONE PINT

**BANANA WAFER PUDDING**
with that *matchless* cooked-in flavor

Prepare pudding as directed on back of package. Chill. Arrange alternate layers of banana slices, vanilla wafers and pudding in a serving dish — finishing with a layer of pudding. Serve with whipped cream. It will be very easy to get the children in for dinner tonight. (And isn't this nice to know: you can create a whole extravaganza of different pies with this extraordinary package, too.)

You did it...

... with Jell-O Pudding and Pie Filling—*the one dessert* that never stops being different.

Jell-O is a registered trade-mark of General Foods Corp.

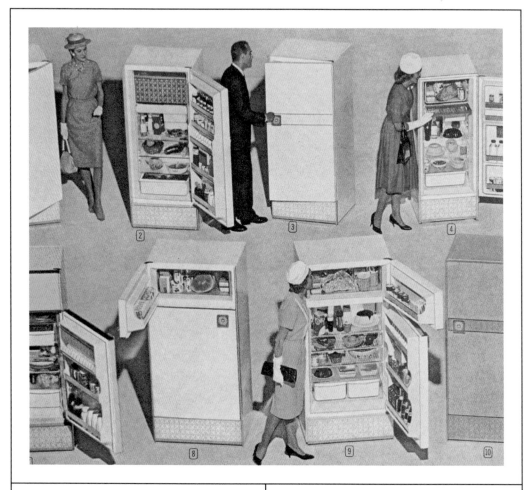

Starches had long been used in textile manufacture, but are now used in making pharmaceuticals, paper, and concrete as well. Guar gum, a product of the guar bean, was once primarily used as a thickener for yoghurts, soups, and ice-cream (it prevents ice-crystal formation when foods containing water are frozen), but is now more likely to be part of the hydraulic fracturing process known as fracking, in which a pressurized liquid thickened with guar gum is injected into the ground to displace deposits of natural gas and oil. West Texas has planted forests of guar trees solely to be used for fracking purposes, but India is by far the world's largest producer, making around three million tons a year for export to the Western world. *Plus ça change.*

We don't even notice it any more, this thickness that we are swimming in: it is as much a part of our post-industrial world as mines and railways. But if someone, someday asks you, in a strange, strangled voice, why all our liquid foods seem so damned thick, you can tell them: it's complicated.

ABOVE | Frigidaire advert. *Better Homes & Gardens*, August 1960. | OPPOSITE | Rowntree's Table Jelly delights, *The Tatler*, 18 July 1928. | OVERLEAF LEFT Cold War-era Philco Electronics advert, featuring a fridge, a satellite and a computer. *Look*, July 1961. OVERLEAF RIGHT | Yuri Gagarin on the front page of Soviet magazine, *Krokodil*, 20 April 1961.

# ROWNTREE'S TABLE JELLY DELIGHTS

RUSSIAN CHARLOTTE

CHOCOLATE BLANCMANGE

JELLY MARLBOROUGH

RASPBERRY POMMES

**Wanted:** A refrigerator that properly preserves many foods under different temperature and humidity conditions ideal for each. The answer is the Philco Custom-Tailored Cold Refrigerator—with a right place, right temperature, right humidity for *every* food. Butter, cheese, milk, eggs, meat, vegetables—even ice, in some models—have a special, scientifically controlled area. And there's no frost to scrape in either the fresh-food compartment or the freezer. Though free-standing, every new Philco is UL-approved for recessed installation, for that <u>custom</u> look without custom cost!

**Philco monitors our first man in space!** The National Aeronautics and Space Administration (NASA) chose 16 Philco TechRep engineers to play important roles in monitoring the electrical and mechanical systems in Project Mercury's first astronaut shot. At many monitoring points around the globe, a Philco TechRep was one of the 3 key men at the vital control consoles. His responsibility: observing the spacecraft's attitude, pitch, roll, yaw motion, fuel, cabin and suit oxygen supply, temperature and pressure—and recommending any corrective earth control measures necessary.

Рисунок И. СЕМЕНОВА.

Ю. А. ГАГАРИН: — Полет продолжается нормально. Состояние невесомости переношу хорошо.

# КРОКОДИЛ

№ 11 (1625)  ГОД ИЗДАНИЯ 39-Й  20 АПРЕЛЯ 1961

PICTURE CREDITS

References in *italic* indicate pages on which illustrations appear

# ACKNOWLEDGEMENTS

I couldn't have done this without the forbearance and encouragement of my family, Mandy, Ena and Cassius.

Thanks to Josh and Matt for steering me onto this track and giving me a spot to park my occasionally fanciful theories, and Jon for making this happen.